Praise f<

"Matt and Melissa created ....rs! *Rock Your Read Aloud* highlights the important and lasting impact reading aloud has on children. They have created such a gift to share with us through Novel Effect, as everyone can 'rock their read-aloud' with this fun and important digital tool."

–Shannon McClintock Miller, District Teacher Librarian,
Van Meter School, Iowa

"In our school district, we are on a mission to inspire the joy of reading in our students as we help them prepare for college, careers, and life. Matt and his team have helped support our mission by developing Novel Effect. The intuitiveness of this resource has made the read-aloud experience not only fun and engaging for the listener, but the reader, too! *Rock Your Read Aloud* is a must-have for anyone looking to make reading an adventure!"

–Jennifer Saunders, Director of Library Media Services,
Atlanta Public Schools

"*Rock Your Read Aloud* is a transformative guide that elevates the way educators, parents, and caregivers connect with young readers. Matt and Melissa Hammersley, with their deep expertise in literacy and technology, offer an innovative and practical roadmap for creating read-aloud sessions that inspire a lifelong love of reading. Their insights make this an invaluable resource for anyone invested in fostering a meaningful connection with children through storytelling."

–Jen Davis Wickens, Founder, Impact Public Schools,
and Co-Founder, Seminar

"For those aspiring to master read-aloud skills, you need this book and its valuable insight. Matt and Melissa emphasize the significance of reading aloud to children through research-backed expertise and practical lesson ideas."

–Blake Hopper, Assistant Principal and
Former School Librarian, Tennessee

ROCK YOUR READ ALOUD

ROCK YOUR READ ALOUD

SPARKING CURIOSITY AND CONFIDENCE IN LITTLE READERS

Matthew and Melissa Hammersley

JB JOSSEY-BASS™
A Wiley Brand

To Willa & Max–You are and always will be our inspiration and joy.

Contents

Preface

The seed for what became Novel Effect was planted while we attended a baby shower, in the time we were awaiting the arrival of our first child. There, Matt witnessed a friend captivating a group of children and parents with animated storytelling–adding silly voices and sound effects that had the children on the edge of theirs seats and the adults laughing and joining in as a chorus. That magical experience, where reading aloud became a shared and immersive event, stayed with us as we approached parenthood.

Novel Effect grew from our desire to recreate that enchanting storytime experience, to help us cultivate in our own children a love of reading that will carry through their lives. We believe reading together for pleasure and ensuring that it creates positive moments and memories is a fundamental part of helping all children develop the interest and motivation necessary to acquire the literacy skills to be not only readers but avid learners and thinkers.

This conviction was so strong that what began as a simple request to family and friends for support in building a library of children's books for our own child became a pivotal moment in our lives. It transformed our careers–from a patent attorney and a graphic designer–into an all-encompassing mission centered on creating impactful literacy experiences.

Educators, librarians, and parents alike consistently express a need for tools and guidance to inspire children to read. Each of us share the dream of placing the right book in a child's hands at the perfect moment, making a significant difference in their lives. However, many children and teenagers today find little meaning in reading, particularly when their attention is pulled so many different directions by video games, technology, and social media, among other distractions.

Although our backgrounds are not in education or library science, we are parents deeply invested in our children's journey toward literacy, as well as in the journeys of countless other young learners. We are dreamers and creators. And, supported by a team of brilliant educators, librarians, musicians, artists, and engineers, we developed the first software of its kind that combines physical children's picture books with advanced speech recognition technology, creating what we call a soundscape—layers of interactive music, character voices, and sound effects that enhance the read-aloud experience.

This tool helps make every read-aloud session magical. The addition of responsive audio, designed to complement the words as they're read aloud and draw attention to the images on the page, make literacy a multisensory, interactive experience. Across homes, classrooms, and school communities worldwide, Novel Effect has been embraced as a vital element in fostering a culture of reading that excites and inspires young learners. Our approach has facilitated millions of dynamic, immersive read-alouds, resulting in increased engagement, understanding, and appreciation of literature among children.

Through these experiences, we have learned that children and their caregivers are most eager to read aloud together when personal connection and joy are at the heart of their reading goals. Effective reading instruction involves a blend of critical elements, and while we will explore these with the support of research and expert insights, this book also shares the invaluable lessons we've gathered on the art of storytelling from educators, parents, and children around the world. We have discovered that the way you tell a story can profoundly motivate a child to embrace books as a means of understanding the world.

The manner in which you read aloud together will leave a lasting impact on both you and the children in your life. When we use literacy as a tool to learn, play, and grow with children of all learning abilities, we are rewarded with the joyful melody of small voices asking to read aloud again.

We are dedicated—in our parenting, our work, and this book—to spread the magic of the read-aloud to children and adults alike, because there is nothing more gratifying than hearing a child, with hopeful eyes and a cherished picture book in hand, say, "Let's read!"

Acknowledgments

We express our deepest gratitude to Catherine Coyle, Tracy Mercier, Matt Boerner, and the entire Novel Effect team for all their unwavering support and efforts throughout this journey. To Tracy Brown Hamilton and Amy Fandrei and the team at Jossey-Bass, who endured our faults and strengthened our passion. And to the millions of teachers, parents, and kids who have made our dreams a reality!

About the Authors

Based in Seattle, Washington, Matt and Melissa are partners in both work as the founders of Novel Effect and in life with two little ones, Max and Willa. They've spent the last ten years immersing themselves in read-alouds at home and in the classroom. They've appeared on the hit TV show *Shark Tank* and reached millions of kids, teachers, and parents in pursuit of their mission: to make reading together magical. Prior to Novel Effect, Matt was a chemical engineering undergrad and became an intellectual property attorney. Melissa's background is in architecture and graphic design, and she owns her own technical illustration business. Together, they've strived to make an impact in the lives of families and classrooms and help all kids discover the love of reading.

Introduction

> "Reading should not be presented to children as a chore,
> a duty. It should be offered as a gift."
>
> *– Kate DiCamillo*

Every week across the world, around three billion people engage in the time-honored tradition of reading aloud together. Parents, grandparents, aunts, uncles, cousins, caregivers, teachers, and librarians all take part. But at the same time, children are often glued to their screens, parents feel overwhelmed, and teachers face immense pressure to boost reading scores. The COVID-19 pandemic has only worsened this decline in reading achievement, despite the valiant efforts of students and educators to adapt to unprecedented challenges.

Consider this: The average first-grade teacher spends about 20 percent of their classroom instruction time reading aloud. Yet, how many college courses actually teach the art of reading aloud and storytelling? Similarly, parents are often advised to read to their children for at least 15 minutes a day—but who teaches them how to do it effectively?

Effective reading instruction encompasses several critical components: phonemic awareness, phonics, fluency, vocabulary, and comprehension. While these cognitive skills are foundational, metacognitive skills, such as comprehension, begin to develop during read-alouds and are crucial for setting a complete foundation for literacy. These soft skills allow readers to grasp deeper meanings—understanding the author's intent, character traits, and motivations. Instilling a lifelong love of reading involves this combination of hard and soft skills, as well as fostering enjoyment and engagement. This is the art we hope to help all users of Novel Effect and readers of this book cultivate, so they can fully reap the rewards of reading.

The Current State of Literacy

It's no surprise that children are falling behind. Across the country, reading scores have dropped, and the test-score gap between students in low-poverty and high-poverty schools has widened by approximately 15 percent. The pandemic disrupted every aspect of life, leaving teachers to conduct lessons virtually, learners to self-regulate at home, and parents to take a more active role in their children's education. While children are resilient, they cannot wait for the situation to improve on its own, especially as school and public libraries are closed due to funding gaps while books are being banned from discussion and removed from shelves. We must guide them through these challenging times, especially in reading and understanding how to access knowledge, which is crucial for success in all subjects and forms the foundation for their future.

Our brains are wired to love stories. Early exposure to books and literacy fosters children's social, emotional, and cognitive growth. Before they can understand the text, the social and emotional connections made during read-alouds are crucial. According to Scholastic's 2023 Rise of the Read-Aloud reading report, eight out of ten children report loving or liking being read aloud to, and four in ten kids aged six to eleven whose parents have stopped reading aloud to them wish their parents had continued.

Reading achievement is closely linked to reading motivation and behavior. Research shows that read-alouds benefit not only young children but also middle-grade students, high schoolers, and even adults. When we consistently come together for read-alouds, we create a shared joy that goes beyond the words and illustrations on the pages. It's about face-to-face connection, shared meaning, and understanding.

In today's world, where distractions are endless, and screens often dominate our attention, we need to create magical moments with our children that support their curiosity and increase their interest in literacy and learning. Our favorite childhood memories often involve being snuggled up with a loved one, reading our favorite books repeatedly. We want all children to experience that same joy and connection with their community of friends and the grown-ups in their lives, with books at the center.

Reading aloud has a profound impact on children's development. It enhances vocabulary, empathy, and attention span. It helps children understand the world around them, shows them the value of reading for pleasure, and fosters a lifelong love of reading. As caregivers, we have the power to make every read-aloud session a magical and memorable experience. This not only benefits our children emotionally and academically, but also creates lasting memories that they will cherish and pass on to their own children.

Building Connections Through Reading Aloud

This is a challenging time for read-alouds. A vocal minority of "concerned parents" has created chaos around the availability of diverse and inclusive books in libraries, schools, and classrooms. Despite this, educators, parents, and children report that diversity in literature is one of the most important decision-making factors they consider when choosing a book from the shelf. According to the same Scholastic report mentioned earlier, 68 percent of parents want diverse literature to read to their children, and 54 percent of children want the same.

We stand firm in our commitment to inspiring a love of reading in every child through diverse and inclusive stories. We celebrate the authors and illustrators who share their experiences and imaginations through their work. We support the librarians, teachers, and educators who awaken a lifelong love of learning in their students in the face of mounting distraction and mistrust.

Every child deserves to see themselves reflected in the pages of a book and to know that their experiences are valid and valued. Books open our minds to new places, experiences, and perspectives. They help us discover who we are and chart our own paths. A well-crafted, well-told story can change lives, and the way you read those stories aloud to a child can have a lasting impact.

How to Read This Book

This book is divided into two parts. Part I explores the science, power, and methodology behind an effective, engaging, and over-all joyful read-aloud, whether you are reading to your own child, a child in your care, or a classroom full of eager, emerging readers. It looks at reading aloud as one of the most important foundations for supporting not only literacy achievement in children, but a life-time love of reading.

We look at the power of the picture book, a genre of literature that is nowhere near as simplistic as it may appear at first glance, but an invaluable resource to introduce the youngest readers—beginning at infancy—to the wonderful world of stories, sharing, and discovering, and, ultimately, learning to read and love books.

Because the soundscapes that accompany our Novel Effect library play such a big role in how the app helps you rock your read-aloud, we've included a chapter on why we think sound enhances emotional understanding during a read-aloud, amping up the big feelings—excitement, sadness, joy, sometimes a bit of fun fright—that readers experience while hearing a story.

Finally we delve into approaches to achieving the goal of this book, and Novel Effect as well: rocking your read-aloud. We offer tips and advice for holding your readers' attention, for increasing engagement and comprehension through open-ended questions and play while you read, as well as other strategies to help both you and your young listeners connect with each other and have fun as you share a book together.

Part II offers book-specific read-aloud lessons that provide suggestions for discussion or activities before, during, and after you read a selected book from our Novel Effect library. Novel Effect app users can scan the QR code on each lesson page to quickly access the soundscape and corresponding worksheets for each title. Alternatively, you can download all the worksheets from www.noveleffect.com/rockyourreadaloud.

Although we intend this book to serve anyone who reads aloud, whether they use Novel Effect or not, we also hope it will spark a curiosity for all to discover the magic of enhancing their regular storytime routine with a soundscape!

While this book focuses on adults reading aloud to children, the benefits are universal across age, race, and other demographics. We invite you to join us in making every read-aloud session a magical experience, enriching the lives of children, creating memories that will last a lifetime, and building motivation so they become avid readers themselves. In fact, as we've seen countless times from children after experiencing their first soundscape, emerging readers will want to read on their own, often right away, to drive the storytelling experience!

Our goal with Novel Effect is both simple yet profound: We want to make reading aloud together a fun activity that children and adults will enjoy and through which they will develop deeper connections. By encouraging and developing a lifelong love of reading in children, we will foster their social, emotional, and cognitive growth, and prepare the next generation to tackle the challenges that undoubtedly lie ahead. We are a team of experts in various fields—including educators, librarians, actors, singers, musicians, engineers—who all share a genuine love and appreciation for children's literature and a commitment to this shared goal and purpose.

Let's celebrate the power of stories and the joy of reading aloud together.

ROCK YOUR READ ALOUD

Part I

THE ART AND SCIENCE OF THE READ ALOUD

The chapters in Part I provide the foundational knowledge behind an effective and joyful read-aloud experience. Here, we explore the science of reading aloud and how it supports not just literacy, but emotional connection and a lifetime love of books. We also discuss the profound power of picture books, which serve as an incredible gateway for young children to explore stories, ideas, and their emotions. Additionally, you'll discover why sound is a vital component in engaging young readers—how the Novel Effect soundscapes enhance emotional depth and amplify the story's impact.

The Magic of the Read Aloud

Children who realize in their first few weeks and months of life that listening to stories is the purest heaven; who understand that books are filled with delights, facts, fun and food for thought; who fall in love with their parents and their parents with them, while stories are being shared; and who are read to for ten minutes a day in their first five years, usually learn to read quickly, happily and easily. And a whole lot of goodness follows for the entire community. No wonder I can't contain myself.

– Mem Fox, from Reading Magic

It is not enough to simply teach children to read; we have to give them something worth reading. Something that will stretch their imaginations—something that will help them make sense of their own lives and encourage them to reach out toward people whose lives are quite different from their own.

– Katherine Patterson

News of a literacy crisis is widespread, and evidenced by many students struggling to achieve proficiency in reading by third grade. It is an even more challenging situation for marginalized students, including those from minority backgrounds, students with disabilities, and multilingual learners, who often face additional barriers to reaching reading proficiency.

Research repeatedly shows that reading aloud together is the single most important thing a caregiver can do for a child to boost their literacy skills. There is a clear connection between reading engagement and reading achievement: Children who read more are better readers and more likely to have academic success. Reading aloud to children early and often will result in the most gains—we began reading regularly to our own children before they were even born—but it is never too late to start a read-aloud routine.

Unfortunately, not all kids are read to in this way before they start Pre-K or kindergarten. School communities and classroom teachers are left to fill in the gaps. Making sure that read-alouds are a planned part of instructional time allows all students to take part in shared literacy experience and gain the benefits to language and background knowledge. This approach is even more effective than sustained silent reading because the burden is removed from the child, and the joy of reading is shared with the entire school or classroom community.

Our mission at Novel Effect may sound ambitious: to have *every* child reading *above* their grade level. We believe this starts by creating experiences that make reading fun for children, so they develop a desire for reading at an early age. Fostering a love for literature at a young age can open up new worlds for children, nurture their imaginations, strengthen their connections to familiar experiences, and build empathy and understanding for the lived experiences of others. Research shows that reading aloud is a cherished and beloved tradition by parents and children. Both express enjoyment in this special time together. This doesn't happen by simply making reading a chore, or only a task to complete; when you read aloud you model the fun and adventure that is possible in a story and unleash the magic of the books.

We believe in making reading aloud fun and magical, captivating children early and helping cultivate a love for books and reading that lasts a lifetime. At the heart of our mission is a desire to build relationships, to connect every child with a community of readers—including parents, teachers, public librarians, and other children—and to empower this community with best in class tools, curriculum, and instruction to develop early literacy skills.

We've seen firsthand how our soundscapes can be game-changers in classrooms. Teachers tell us frequently that their effect is like magic—it grabs student's attention and helps them connect with the story on a deeper level. We love hearing stories about how using soundscapes (the subject of Chapter 3) to enhance a story doesn't just keep children engaged; it helps them understand and feel the emotions behind the words, and it makes stories accessible to every child.

We want every teacher to experience a read-aloud where both you and your students are completely lost in the fun, silliness, and emotion of a story together—to discover and share the pure joy of the read-aloud. It doesn't matter how many times you've read the story; the magic is always there because of the connections to your emotions, your experiences, and the adventures that await. In this chapter, we describe the benefits of reading aloud to children—not just to better their chances for academic success but to enrich their experience with literature and with their reading community.

Reading as a Social Act

Early education prioritizes literacy skills to establish the foundation for a lifetime of learning. Children who cannot read well will fail to grasp important concepts and miss educational milestones, with compounding consequences. The way we approach achieving literacy goals can be complex and different for every student. Learning to read can often be thought of as a primarily—and often frustrating to learn—cognitive skill (more on this in Chapter 4), that requires explicit systemic instruction. But developing a love for reading in a child requires emotional skills to help children comprehend what they are reading, or hearing read to them.

Reading aloud is more than just a pedagogical tool; it is a social act that fosters connections, nurtures emotional bonds, and entertains us. When we read together we create a shared pool of knowledge and ideas that bind us with each other as well as larger communities. And it is also social in the sense of thinking and learning about "big ideas"—anything from emotional understanding, values and ethical behavior, or diversity and cultural awareness—that form your perceptions about these big ideas, locally and globally.

Our philosophy is that a lifetime of literacy doesn't grow by treating reading as a solitary activity. Reading alone and even listening to an audiobook or recording of a book being read can support literacy skills, yes. But reading aloud together is where the real connection, thinking, and learning takes place. It provides a chance to build bonds, share stories, spark conversations, develop reading comprehension skills, and most importantly, have fun together. And it's definitely not just about the child's enjoyment; it's also about creating a fulfilling experience for the adult reader.

As author and literary editor Emilie Buchwald widely is credited with saying, "Children are made readers on the laps of their parents." And as children grow, the impact of being read to continues to grow as well: Even when a child may not yet be able to read the words themselves or even understand them all, having a book read with them helps them grasp what reading is actually about. They begin to connect with the meaning behind the words on the page. This, we believe, will not only help a child ultimately develop skills to read on their own, but provide an additional impetus that they will be more likely to want to read, and to read often.

The following sections explore some of the many benefits of reading together with a child—before *and* after they can read on their own.

Bonding Through Books in the Classroom

Regularly reading aloud to your students can significantly strengthen your relationship with them—and theirs to you. Forging this connection is one of the most important things you can do to positively influence their literacy development, and reading aloud at a predictable, scheduled time that fits into your daily routines in the classroom provides something consistent that they can look forward to.

Having a shared activity like reading also gives you and your students something to talk about, which supports the development of reading and writing skills. Through picture books, students learn about themselves and their classmates as they discuss individual and shared experiences, emotional connections, and perspectives. And children's books often serve as springboards for meaningful conversations about a variety of topics, helping to develop their critical thinking skills (more on that in Chapter 2).

For example, when reading together a book like *After the Fall*, students learn about risk-taking and perseverance. Texts like this invite conversations and enable children to learn about each other's fears, struggles, hopes, and goals. Read-alouds like these tap into empathy and create an environment where they not only better understand each other, but can support each other.

Connecting and Creating Experiences

At their core, books enable children to understand concepts without necessarily experiencing them firsthand, and without feeling the burden of "learning" so much as the pleasure of discovering. Reading to children exposes them to a wide range of subjects and ideas, building their understanding of humanity and the world around them. Over time, reading together can lead to discussions about real-life experiences and issues that might not otherwise arise.

Through picture books, they not only expand their world, but develop understanding and empathy. For example, when reading books like *The Girl Who Thought in Pictures* or *Emanuel's Dream*, children learn about the experiences of people who live with a disability. Learning about others through picture books enables children to apply that information when meeting new people or solving real-world problems.

Benefits to You, the Teacher

When it comes to reading aloud with children, we often focus on them and the benefits they reap. But let's not overlook the adults in the room—the ones holding the book, infusing the words with life, and sharing in the magic of storytelling. You need to be having fun, too.

Think back to those moments when you and your students were engrossed in a tale, swept away by the laughter, the silliness, and the heartfelt moments. That's what we aim for in every read-aloud—inspiring the children to experience the pure joy of the story. And the best part? It never gets old, no matter how many times you've read the same story.

We frequently hear from educators how much fun it is to read aloud books like *Dragons Love Tacos*, *The Book with No Pictures*, or *The Big Cheese*. The books themselves are delightful, and with the additional layer of music and sound effects, it elevates the fun. Teachers giggle at fun puns, bop to catchy background music, and even are surprised by silly sound effects. They get to focus on the pure enjoyment of reading because Novel Effect is doing the performance work.

Building a Foundation for Future Reading Development

Being read to helps children develop essential reading skills, such as print concepts, even before they can decode words themselves, or fully understand their meaning. As children are hearing new words, and especially if they are having conversations about it, before, during, and after the read-aloud is finished, they are building the vocabulary around the book's ideas, expanding their capacity for language and their use of language.

Many literacy coaches and educators encourage you to re-read your students' favorite book as many times as they want, to reinforce vocabulary and aid in language development. This can often encourage children to want to read the book themselves, whether they are truly reading the words or are enjoying the pictures and familiarity of the book. This promotes positive associations with books and reading.

Books like *Last Stop on Market Street*, *Owl Moon*, and *Eyes That Kiss in the Corners* are rich with figurative language. Inferring is a crucial skill in helping children understanding its meaning. With Novel Effect's perfectly timed music, sound effects, and character lines, they make these abstract ideas concrete for them. The same is true when reading stories like *Trombone Shorty*, where the sound-scape music helps students understand what jazz sounds like and the energy felt when he's playing. Reading aloud with stories like these builds background knowledge and develops vocabulary in a supportive way, equipping children with the information needed the next time they come across a similar phrase, event, or time period.

This foundational understanding is crucial for their future reading development, as it introduces them to vocabulary, expands their language skills, and helps them grasp the concept that printed words carry meaning.

Moving Beyond Decoding

Many teachers will be familiar with the concept that by fourth grade, literacy development moves beyond "learning to read" to "reading to learn." Making that transition requires a foundation in comprehension, which we believe only develops in young readers who have discovered an enjoyment rather than a rudimentary skill in reading.

While decoding is undoubtedly essential in developing reading skills, reading itself is about more than that; it involves comprehension, interpretation, and the ability to engage with texts on a deeper level, transforming reading from a mechanical process into a rich and meaningful experience. This is how we develop not only better readers but better thinkers, dreamers, and citizens of the world.

And that's because reading is so much more than just sounding out words on a page; it's about understanding and connecting with the text, developing critical thinking skills, and fostering a genuine love of learning. In the words of Frederick Douglass: "Once you learn to read, you will be forever free."

A member of our team–a former film music composer and software developer who now leads our soundscapes development department–compares learning to read to learning to play music: If you focus on the rudimentary skills–like how to put your hand in the right position on the piano and do whatever is necessary to make a note come out—there's a certain satisfaction in being able to do that. It's kind of fun to take notes on sheet music and make a sound in the real world via this mechanical mechanism of the piano.

But that initial satisfaction wears off quickly. Ultimately, it is about *making music*. Just like when reading, you're making meaning from text on the page. The act of sounding out and decoding the text might be interesting while you're learning, but once you've mastered that, or if you find it hard and don't enjoy it, you need a motivation to continue. If you want to understand the meaning of a book, that's where you'll find the desire to work a little harder, sound it out, and decode it.

When you read aloud to a child, you have the opportunity to introduce new world knowledge, such as vocabulary they would not encounter in their daily lives or the ability to empathize with a character or situation by making a connection to a time they had a similar experience or feeling. As described in Chapter 6, you can incorporate voice inflection, placing emphasis on key words; pacing strategies that help build excitement, hint toward danger, or give weight to sadder moments. You can create silences. You bring the story to life; you make it memorable and meaningful—for you and for the child.

Getting Inside a Book

In her TED Talk, "Why We Should All Be Reading Aloud to Children," teacher, literacy consultant, and performer Rebecca Bellingham relays her experience adapting and directing a production of *Charlotte's Web* with a group of third graders at PS 220, the Mott Haven Village School in the South Bronx.

To engage the children and introduce the story, she began by reading aloud the first chapter from EB White's classic book, in which—as you may recall—young Fern saves a runt pig, whom she names Wilbur, from being slaughtered by her farmer father.

Fern begs her father not to kill the pig:

> *"Please don't kill it," she sobbed, "It's unfair."*
> *Mr. Arable stopped walking. "Fern," he said gently, "you will have to learn to control yourself."*
> *"Control myself?" yelled Fern, "This is a matter of life and death, and you talk about controlling myself?"*

Fern's pleading works, and the pig is saved. At breakfast, Fern sees a carton on her chair:

> *As she approached her chair, the carton wobbled, and there was a scratching noise. Fern looked at her father, then she lifted the lid of the carton. There, inside, looking up at her was the newborn pig. It was a white one. The morning light shone through its ears, turning them pink.*
> *"He is yours," said Mr. Arable, "Saved from an untimely death. And may the good Lord forgive me for this foolishness."*
> *Fern couldn't take her eyes off the tiny pig "Oh!" she whispered, "Oh! Look at him! He is absolutely perfect."*
> *She closed the carton carefully, first she kissed her father, then she kissed her mother, then she opened the lid again, lifted the pig out and held it against her cheek.*

When the chapter was finished, Belligham recalls, her reading had been so engaging, so effectively dramatic, that at least one child was hooked: "Well, when I finished reading the chapter," she says, "the kids lined up for lunch, and a little boy named Joey tugged at my sleeve, and he said, 'Miss B, I felt like I was right there. Like, I could really see that little pig. I never got inside a book before like that.'"

What a wonderful way to express the joy of reading: getting *inside* a book!

That's the power of a read-aloud done well: You grab a child's attention, hook them into the story, and you've opened up a whole new world for them.

Keeping Children Engaged During a Read-Aloud

Keeping students in a classroom engaged during a read-aloud takes a conscious effort. Although stories have an amazing power to grab the emotions and imagination of children and adults like, it can sometimes be hard to compete with all the distractions that surround us. And, naturally, the adult should be engaged and having a good time, too. How do we make sure every child stays hooked and tuned in?

Our approach is all about making reading fun and interactive (much more on this in Chapters 3 and 6). We believe if children enjoy what they're hearing, they'll not only pay attention but also dive deep into the story.

When kids are excited about what they're reading or the stories they are hearing, learning naturally follows. That's why we're so dedicated to equipping teachers with practical ways to make reading sessions full of wonder and excitement. Part II offers many lessons that correspond to nearly 1,000 (and growing) soundscapes on the Novel Effect app.

Read-alouds are filled with wonder and excitement when done well. Soundscapes add an additional layer that helps young readers tune into the ways words leap off the page, notice details they may otherwise miss, and even surprise them. Teachers tell us how well this is achieved when reading aloud with Novel Effect. Students will hear a cat meow and that helps them notice the creature on the page. They'll hear Squirrel say something silly in *The Leaf Thief* and they'll better understand how he's not understanding seasons. They'll hear a fun doorbell in a story like *Pete the Cat: Trick or Pete* and sit up just a bit straighter, lean in just a bit closer so they can pay better attention to what will come next in the story.

Novel Effect soundscapes are interactive by nature, they break down vocabulary, uncover tone, and support character development. Going beyond the story and incorporating interactive strategies during a read-aloud strengthens student understanding and peer relationships.

It's also important to keep things interactive. All kids need to get up and move, all kids need to talk to each other, and all that's part of building understanding and comprehension. Getting kids up and moving, letting them talk about what they're hearing–these are all ways to keep the energy up and make sure every child feels involved. When children can discuss the story and interact with it, they're not just passive listeners; they're active participants in their own learning.

Talking to others helps them clarify their own ideas, challenge their own assumptions, and broadens their perspective. Facilitating conversations amongst students benefits their development of social skills, but also helps them to intuitively strengthen, revise, expand upon, and reconstruct their own ideas. It supports their ability to access and understand the text.

Incorporating movement during a read-aloud not only supports comprehension (depending on how its used), but also activates the brain, awakens it, and makes it alert to attend to others' ideas. For example, when reading aloud *Happy Dreamer*, students can stand up every time they hear a dream that resonates with them. Making read-aloud a multisensory experience with soundscapes, movement, and conversation enriches it, deepens understanding of both simple and complex themes, and just makes it more enjoyable.

Maintaining the attention of young readers' is about creating a safe learning environment that honors their current skill levels while gently pushing them beyond their comfort zone so they are comfortable grappling with big ideas.

Holding an audience of young readers' attention is about creating an environment where stories come alive, and where children feel the adult is equally enthusiastic about the experience. In doing so, we not only keep children engaged while hearing a story, but we help make read-alouds a part of the day children look forward to and truly enjoy.

Teaching Deaf and Hard of Hearing Students with Novel Effect: An Interview with Gina Gardella Ditrio

Gina Gardella Ditrio works in the Norwalk Public School District in Connecticut, where she uses Novel Effect to support deaf and hard of hearing children. Here, she shares with us how Novel Effect has shown results in her teaching, including increasing the enjoyment for children during read-alouds and improving focus. As one second grader told her, "It made me pay attention better."

Note this interview has been edited for length, but you can find the complete version on our blog at noveleffect.com.

Novel Effect: Can you tell us about your work with Novel Effect?

I teach deaf and hard of hearing children, from birth to 14, in the public school system. I travel from school to school, using lots of environmental sounds with my students. I used to carry a big bag of instruments—shakers, clappers, drums. Then Audra Good purchased Novel Effect for Brookside Elementary, and I was like, "Oh my God, this is a game changer." Now I just carry my speakers.

For example, at St. Vincent's Special Needs School, I do group lessons with severely disabled students. I have a disco ball with a speaker so the visually impaired children can zoom in on the light and sound.

That's amazing! What are some of the biggest challenges you face, and how has Novel Effect helped?

With Novel Effect, attention spans have greatly improved, and students are more engaged in read-alouds. YouTube and videos have made it hard for them to enjoy traditional reading. But with Novel Effect, students from age three and up have really improved. Even in my birth to three program, toddlers are more attentive. They sit and listen, even if only for a minute, which is better than without it.

Have there been times where Novel Effect has had a major impact on your teaching style?

Definitely. I have a preschooler I work with in a very distracting environment. With Novel Effect, I can pause the story, ask him questions, and keep him engaged. The sound effects help maintain his focus.

That's so cool! We've heard you had a great experience with a second-grade class as well.

Yes, I read *The Little Old Lady Who Was Not Afraid of Anything* to a second-grade class. One boy told his classmates to be quiet so they could hear the sound effects. Afterward, they said it was the best story ever because they could hear and think about it better. A second grader even said, "It made me pay attention better."

That's wonderful. How do teachers react when you bring Novel Effect into their classrooms?

They love it! One teacher even said her students are fascinated when she reads with it. Audra Good wants me to talk to all the teachers at a staff meeting because of how excited I am about it.

Have you seen a major impact on a particular student with Novel Effect?

Yes, I work with a student with bilateral hearing loss who struggled to follow directions. When I introduced Novel Effect, he stopped, listened, and followed along with the book. It was a game changer for him.

How does Novel Effect work for students with unilateral hearing loss?

It's challenging because they can't locate the sound. I hide the speaker and play Hide 'n' Seek listening games. For kids with bone-anchored hearing aids (BAHA), Novel Effect encourages them to bring their aids to hear better on both sides.

To close, do you have any favorite stories from Novel Effect?

I love the holiday stories, the *There Was an Old Lady* series, and *Big Red Barn*. *The Little Old Lady Who Was Not Afraid of Anything* is a favorite among all my students, from age three to fourteen. I love every single one I read!

Up Next...

This chapter began with a wonderful quote by the extraordinary children's author and literacy expert Mem Fox, so it's perhaps fitting that we close with the same. In her seminal work, *Reading Magic*, she describes a read-aloud experience with a child she had just met, as part of a segment on an Australian television program—it summarizes perfectly how magical a read-aloud can be, for children and adults alike:

> But the most important truth, I believe, is what happened between me and the child. There was a frenzy of silliness and excited game playing, with me shouting and laughing and saying, "Yes! Yes! Yes!" in higher and higher tones, and hugging Ben, who was laughing and grinning as if this "reading" thing were just about the best fun he'd ever had. We were literally rolling around on the floor and banging the book with our hands at each new revelation of its "It's time for bed," shrieking in triumph as the words were revealed on each page.
>
> We were never tense. We were never quiet. Even when we were looking for and finding the same farm animals in each book, we were noisy and wild in our discoveries—and in our togetherness.[1]

Learning to turn your read-alouds into meaningful fun that excites a young reader is something we believe everyone can do. And it starts with something the Novel Effect team has a deep appreciation for: the rich, thought-inspiring medium of children's books, the subject of the next chapter.

---

[1]Mem Fox, *Reading Magic: Why Reading Aloud to Our Children Will Change Their Lives Forever* (New York: Harcourt, 2001), chap. 3, 3, e-book.

Unleashing the Power of the Picture Book

A picture book is text, illustrations, total design; an item of manufacture and a commercial product; a social, cultural, historical document; and, foremost, an experience for a child.

As an artform, it hinges on the interdependence of pictures and words, on the simultaneous display of two facing pages, and on the drama of the turning of the page.

On its own terms its possibilities are limitless.
— *Barbara Bader*, American Picturebooks from Noah's Ark to the Beast Within

A children's story that can only be enjoyed by children is not a good children's story in the slightest.
— *C.S. Lewis*

We have a dual mission at Novel Effect: to guide children in learning to read above grade level and also in learning to love to read. Our philosophy is, if you love to read, you'll want to read more. And this begins with providing young children a wealth of literature that is thought-provoking and meaningful.

Far from simplistic, modern children's literature, when done well, is an art form. With words carefully selected and merged with rich illustrations, picture books are wonderfully accessible and complex in ideas, themes, and perspectives. Think of a character who experiences firsthand big change and adaptation, finding joy in new circumstances, and accepting the journey of life (*The Yellow Bus* by Loren Long) or a sour grape who learns to accept responsibility and forgive (*The Sour Grape* by Jory John)—both of which are part of our soundscape library. But this isn't how it always was.

All readers, from child to adult, who have fallen in love with reading in the modern era, owe a debt to Ursula Nordstrom, an instrumental figure in the evolution of children's literature and publishing. As the editor-in-chief of Harper & Row's Department of Books for Boys and Girls from 1940 to 1973, Nordstrom was known for her unconventional approach: centering the feelings and imagination of children in the books written for them, rather than pushing the values and morals of their parents. She nurtured and publishing groundbreaking works by authors such as E.B. White, Maurice Sendak, Crocket Johnson, Margaret Wise Brown, and Shel Silverstein.

Luckily for us, Nordstrom believed in the power of picture books and had high standards when it came to publishing them. "A good picture book should be fresh, original, and believable," she said. "It should deal with ideas that are familiar to children, and yet provide a new way of looking at those ideas. Above all, it should respect the intelligence and feelings of its young readers."[1]

Throughout her career, Nordstrom advocated that children's reading experiences should never be under-thought or oversimplified. She asserted, "We must assume that our children have a certain amount of good taste and not give them badly written or badly illustrated books just because they are children." She expressed the belief that books for children should honor their intelligence and feelings, reflecting her deep connection to the experience of being a child herself.

At Novel Effect, every member of our team shares this deep appreciation and respect for the picture book as the cornerstone of children's literature, and an equal respect for the child audience. Picture books serve as the entry point into the world of

---

[1]Ursula Nordstrom, *Dear Genius: The Letters of Ursula Nordstrom*, ed. Leonard S. Marcus (New York: HarperCollins, 1998).

reading, laying the foundation for lifelong literacy and a love for storytelling.

In this chapter, we will explore the evolution of children's literature from early "readers," which primarily served to teach children how to read, to the rich and diverse array of books available for children today that foster a deep love of reading. We will also introduce strategies for unlocking the power of the picture book, the focus of our work, which you can put into practice as you explore the read-aloud lessons in Part II of this book.

Looking at Early Children's "Readers"

While early children's readers were primarily designed to teach reading and impart moral lessons, there has (thankfully!) been a significant shift towards creating books that are enjoyable, emotionally engaging, and reflective of the diverse communities children live in and the experiences they have. Nordstrom understood early what we have come to know today: Children are more interested in reading books with characters that look and sound like them.

Many children's books before the mid-twentieth century were heavily didactic, aiming to teach moral lessons or proper behavior. They often focused on instilling virtues such as obedience, hard work, and piety. Examples include the works of authors like Horatio Alger and the "McGuffey Readers," which were used extensively in American schools. These books were designed to shape young minds with clear moral lessons and appropriate behavior, emphasizing obedience, honesty, and other virtues considered essential for young readers at the time.

Children's books from this era often portrayed an idealized and sanitized version of life. They avoided complex or potentially upsetting topics, preferring to present a simplistic and often unrealistic view of the world. This lack of realism meant that the stories rarely addressed the nuanced and sometimes difficult realities of children's lives. Instead, they painted a rosy picture, shielding young readers from the harsher aspects of existence.

The subject matter of these early children's books was typically limited to safe, traditional topics. Stories often revolved around fairy tales, folklore, or historical events with clear, unambiguous morals. There was little room for exploring the emotional and psychological experiences of children. This limited subject matter kept the narratives straightforward and predictable, missing opportunities to delve into the rich inner lives of young readers and the complexities of their feelings and experiences.

The language used in children's readers was generally very simple and straightforward, sometimes underestimating the intelligence and emotional depth of young readers. This simplicity often resulted in narratives that failed to challenge or engage children on a deeper level. Illustrations, if present, were often rudimentary and served merely as decorative accompaniments to the text. They did little to enhance or expand on the story, functioning primarily as visual aids rather than integral components of the storytelling.

Books from this period also reinforced traditional gender roles, with boys depicted as adventurous and brave, while girls were shown as passive and domestic. This gender stereotyping limited the kinds of stories that could be told and the characters that could be represented. Boys were the heroes of daring exploits, while girls were confined to the home, reflecting societal expectations and norms of the time. This reinforcement of gender roles shaped young readers' perceptions of what was possible and appropriate for their gender.

However, as societal norms and educational philosophies evolved, so did children's literature. There has been a significant shift toward creating books that are enjoyable, emotionally engaging, and reflective of diverse experiences. Modern children's books often tackle complex and realistic topics, encouraging children to think critically about the world around them. They explore a wide range of themes, including diversity, inclusion, and emotional well-being. This evolution in children's literature reflects a broader understanding of child development and the importance of addressing the emotional and psychological needs of young readers.

The following sections take a closer look at what was typically available to young readers historically.

Seventeenth to Eighteenth Centuries

Up until the eighteenth century, educational tools and literature for children in the United States were primarily designed to teach basic literacy and instill moral and religious values. Here are some notable examples from this period:

- **Hornbooks (used in England as early as the 15th century and introduced to New England during the 1600s):** One of the earliest educational tools, hornbooks were wooden paddles with printed sheets of the alphabet, numbers, and prayers, mounted on a paddle and protected by a thin, clear layer of animal horn or mica, held in place by brass strips to keep the sheet safe.
- **The New England Primer (late 1600s):** Widely used in American colonies, this book combined the alphabet with moral and religious lessons, aiming to instill Christian values.

McGuffey Readers (Nineteenth Century)

In the nineteenth century, educational literature for children continued to evolve, with a greater emphasis on structured learning and moral education. Notable works from this period include the McGuffey Readers. Created by William Holmes McGuffey, these were among the first textbooks designed for different grade levels. They included a mix of moral lessons, reading exercises, and excerpts from literature, aiming to teach reading while imparting ethical and moral values. Also called Eclectic Readers, these books combined literature, poems, and informational texts with moral lessons and were used extensively in American schools.

The "Dick and Jane" Era (1930s to 1970s)

During this era, named after a popular series of children's "readers," the primary goal was to teach children how to read, using a "look-say" method where students would memorize whole words through repeated exposure. The stories were simple and depicted idealized, middle-class American life.

The Dick and Jane Series, developed by William S. Gray and Zerna Sharp and published by Scott, Foresman and Company, became iconic in American education from the 1930s to the 1970s. The books featured simple, repetitive text with a controlled vocabulary, designed to teach reading through sight words and basic phonics.

While effective in teaching basic reading skills, the Dick and Jane series was often criticized for its lack of diversity and for presenting a very narrow, stereotypical view of American life.

Shift Towards Literature for Enjoyment

From the 1950s onwards, influential figures like Ursula Nordstrom began to push for children's books that were not just instructional but also enjoyable and emotionally engaging. This period saw the publication of many classic children's books that focused on storytelling, character development, and emotional depth.

Books like *Charlotte's Web* by E.B. White and *Where the Wild Things Are* by Maurice Sendak offered rich narratives that could engage children's imaginations and emotions, marking a shift from a reliance on purely instructional texts to RICH literature that children could enjoy and connect with on a deeper level.

Modern Era

Today's children's literature used in schools includes a wide range of genres and topics, emphasizing diversity, inclusion, and social-emotional learning.

How We Select Books for the Novel Effect Soundscape Library

Novel Effect's Dynamic, Diverse, and Engaging Library

Judy Blume said, "Let children read whatever they want and then talk about it with them. If parents and kids can talk together, we won't have as much censorship because we won't have as much fear."[2]

We have an unwavering support for diverse and inclusive storytelling. We celebrate authors and illustrators who share their unique experiences through their written works.

Our library is meticulously curated with the consultation of educators and on-staff librarians who select books that are timely, relevant, and deeply engaging. Each book is carefully considered for its ability to spark meaningful conversations, evoke emotional responses, or prompt curiosity in young readers, and our soundscapes team takes great thought in complementing the text, deepening comprehension, and sustaining children's interest throughout the reading session (more on this in Chapter 3).

Importantly, though, our selection process begins in the requests made by the thousands of teachers, parents, and children who use the app. We sort through tens of thousands of requests each month to find the next perfect read-aloud everyone will be clamoring to get their hands on. We analyze the top requests and dive into the stories. We look for great writing, great lessons, and a story that can be enhanced by a soundscape.

We are also committed to diversity, offering a wide range of titles for various age groups and developmental stages. From preschoolers learning basic concepts to older children exploring complex themes, our library ensures inclusivity and representation for all readers to ensure every classroom and family will find the perfect book for them.

With nearly 1,000 stories (and growing!) in our collection and new additions weekly, we strive to provide a dynamic and engaging library. Our goal is to foster a lifelong love of reading among children, support educators in their literacy initiatives, and support families in building those initial literacy foundations.

---

[2]Judy Blume, "On Censorship," Judy Blume's website, accessed October 30, 2024, https://www.judyblume.com/hcensorship.php.

Unlocking the Power of the Modern Picture Book!

The tools children once used to learn to read were rigid and limited, but their intent was fundamental: to teach essential literacy skills. While our perspectives and materials have thankfully expanded (goodbye, hornbooks!), the core goal of children's reading materials–to impart literacy and foster understanding of the world–remains unchanged.

Today, we have a vast array of books and stories to share, created by an increasingly diverse and imaginative community of authors and illustrators. Modern picture books, with their wide range of perspectives, characters, and voices, have transformed children's literature into an art form that not only entertains but also serves as a powerful tool for adults. These stories can help guide meaningful conversations between adults and children about complex or sensitive topics, offering valuable insights for readers of all ages.

Children are naturally drawn to the visual cues in picture books, which help convey emotions, actions, and settings. This makes it easier and more enjoyable for them to understand and engage with the text. Picture books introduce young readers to a diverse vocabulary beyond daily language, helping them connect words to their meanings–a critical skill in language development.

These books are invaluable for fostering language skills and a love for reading. Their engaging narratives, vivid illustrations, and interactive formats inspire imagination, promote comprehension, and empower children to explore literature. By blending captivating visuals with engaging text, picture books enhance both comprehension and vocabulary acquisition.

The following sections explore the many ways picture books engage, entertain, and inspire young readers, emphasizing their role in early literacy development and fostering a deep connection to the joys of storytelling. Here's how good picture books play a significant role in nurturing young minds and shaping their lifelong appreciation for literature.

Contextual Learning Through Images and Text

Picture books harness the power of visual storytelling to provide essential context that aids in faster word comprehension and vocabulary expansion. Illustrations not only support what the text explicitly says, but also expand upon it and enrich the story. The combination of vibrant illustrations and accompanying text allows children to visually connect words with their meanings, facilitating a deeper understanding of language concepts from an early age. This immersive experience not only builds vocabulary but also prompts curiosity and engagement in young readers.

Developing Phonological Awareness Through Rhyme

The rhythmic patterns and rhymes found in picture books play a pivotal role in developing phonological awareness–the ability to recognize and manipulate sounds within words. Through playful rhymes and repetitive phrases, children refine their listening skills and grasp the fundamental building blocks of language. These linguistic patterns not only make reading enjoyable but also lay a strong foundation for future literacy skills by enhancing auditory discrimination and comprehension.

Sequencing and Storytelling Clarity

Understanding story sequence is vital for comprehension, and picture books excel in making narrative flow tangible through clear, sequential illustrations. By visually depicting the progression of events, children learn to sequence story elements cohesively, which strengthens their ability to comprehend and follow stories effectively. This structured approach encourages children to engage with narratives critically and fosters a deeper appreciation for storytelling dynamics.

Encouraging Visual Thinking and Imagination

Visual elements in picture books serve dual purposes by facilitating comprehension and stimulating visual thinking. Illustrations provide visual cues that aid in recalling earlier story events, thereby fostering comprehension and contextual understanding. These vivid images charge children's imaginations, encouraging them to explore and interpret story settings, characters, and themes creatively. This visual engagement not only enhances the reading experience but also nurtures critical thinking and problem-solving skills.

Encouraging Engagement and Interaction

Picture books are designed to captivate young readers with their colorful illustrations and accessible language. Their easy-to-follow format invites frequent pauses for discussion, enabling adults to interact with children and deepen their comprehension of the story. These discussions not only enhance understanding but also cultivate crucial communication skills, preparing children for academic success and lifelong learning.

Building a Foundation for Literacy

Regardless of a child's age or literacy level, picture books serve as an ideal introduction to reading. Through their visually appealing format and engaging narratives, these books instill a love for storytelling from an early age, nurturing a lifelong appreciation for literature. By immersing children in the joy of reading, picture books pave the way for continued exploration of diverse genres and themes, fostering a rich literary experience that extends beyond childhood.

Enhancing Listening Skills and Language Acquisition

By combining visual and auditory cues, picture books enhance children's listening skills and reinforce comprehension. Children can follow the story visually while listening to the text, which strengthens their ability to understand spoken language and interpret story nuances. This multisensory approach not only supports language development but also fosters a deeper connection to the narrative, making reading a multisensory and enriching experience.

Fostering Critical Thinking Through Cause and Effect

Picture books effectively teach cause and effect relationships by presenting story events clearly and accessibly. Through guided discussions that emphasize causal connections, children learn to identify and understand the consequences of characters' actions within the narrative context. This critical thinking skill promotes deeper comprehension and encourages children to make connections between story elements and real-world scenarios, enhancing their overall cognitive development.

Developing Story Structure Awareness

Finally, picture books help children develop a foundational understanding of story structure—recognizing the beginning, middle, and end of narratives. While this is particularly true for early and emerging readers, picture books for older readers often introduce more complex story structures, such as the five-point story arc. Engaging with these diverse narratives allows children to analyze deeper themes, character motivations, and conflicts.

Research shows that as children age, they are read aloud to less frequently, despite strong evidence that reading aloud should continue beyond age five or six as they develop more advanced literacy skills. By encouraging teachers of older students to incorporate picture books and read-alouds, we can expand our reach and foster a deeper appreciation for storytelling dynamics across grade levels, helping to build strong, lifelong readers.

Bridging Worlds Through Art

Picture books are incredibly well suited to helping kids connect their personal experiences with bigger stories about themselves and the world. Jessica Mantei and Lisa Kervin, who teach at the University of Wollongong in Australia, looked into this in their study "Interpreting the images in a picture book: Students make connections to themselves, their lives, and experiences."[3]

Mantei and Kervin talk about "funds of knowledge," which are important skills and ideas that kids learn from their families and communities. These cultural insights are often ignored in traditional schooling but can really boost learning when teachers include them in lessons.

Their research, focusing on books like Jeannie Baker's *Mirror*, shows how these stories with pictures can connect what kids learn at home with what they learn at school. When kids make art in response to these books, they show how much they connect personally, which isn't always easy with regular assignments.

Mantei and Kervin say that schools often focus too much on writing as the main way to show what kids know. They think schools should pay more attention to what kids can express through different ways, like drawing and telling stories with pictures. This kind of teaching can make classrooms feel more welcoming and help kids understand books better while linking what they learn at home and school.

By using good children's books and art together, they say, teachers can get kids excited, help them imagine new things, and get into deeper ideas. This isn't just about learning school stuff—it's about respecting and building on what each kid brings to class, from their own background and culture.

---

[3]Jessica Mantei and Lisa Kervin, "Interpreting the Images in a Picture Book: Students Make Connections to Themselves, Their Lives and Experiences," *English Teaching: Practice and Critique* 13, no. 2 (2014): 76–92.

A Beautiful, Artful World: The Synergy of Words and Pictures

Picture books are so called because, obviously, they contain illustrations (not all children's books do, of course, such as *The Book with No Pictures* by B.J. Novak, also a popular soundscape). The art in children's books works harmoniously with the text to create a rich, immersive experience. The images not only complement the narrative but also help in conveying emotions, settings, and actions that words alone might not fully capture. This link between words and images engages young readers' imaginations, aiding in comprehension and retention of the story.

For example, another story in our library, *A Hat for Minerva Louise* by Janet Morgan Stoeke, is a charming story that is greatly supported by its illustrations, which provide essential context and enhance the narrative. The story is simple: Minvera Lousie searches for a hat and eventually finds one that fits her head perfectly. The text alone does not reveal the most important details: that Minerva Louise is a chicken and that the hat is actually a glove. These details are vividly conveyed through the illustrations though never mentioned in the text.

The synergy between words and images in the book aids in the understanding of emotions, actions, and overall comprehension of the story. And when read in tandem with our soundscape for this and all titles in our library, additional layers of understanding and enjoyment are possible. They also make books more accessible: One educator particularly highlighted the Minvera Louise soundscape when sharing the story with a sight-impaired student. The addition of chicken noises and other sound effects enabled the student to correctly answer comprehension questions about the book. This success highlights how sound can convey information that would otherwise be inaccessible, such as the identity of Minerva Louise as a chicken.

Illustrations can also introduce children to art appreciation, enhancing their visual literacy. As Jane Doonan eloquently writes in her book, *Looking at Pictures in Picture Books*: "When we hold a picture book, we have in our hands a pictured world full of ideas. We play with these ideas and play with our own ideas around the pictured world. The more skillful we are, and the more ideas the picture book contains, the more the ideas go on bouncing. And in the process, we create something of our very own."[4]

When children—or we—read a picture book, our brains switch back and forth from the words to the accompanying illustrations, in equal measure. The words give us sounds and expectations; the illustrations fulfill these, and in combination the story comes to life. That connection between word and image is the magic of the picture book.

With picture books, the two media—language and image—engage so closely that the story cannot be told fully without either being present. Celebrated children's book author Elaine Moss said, "You don't have to tell the story in the words. You can come out of the words and into the pictures and you get this nice kind of antiphonal fugue effect." Moss, a strong advocate for children's literacy, also succinctly believed that "only real books can produce real readers."[5]

Up Next . . .

Picture books can have a profound impact on childhood development and literacy. From sparking curiosity and empathy to nurturing a lifelong love for storytelling, these books serve as foundational tools in every child's development as a reader—and can encourage them to want to share stories of their own, through words, pictures, or both.

The next chapter gets to the heart of Novel Effect, our soundscapes. These thoughtfully composed and voiced recordings—each uniquely created for every individual book in our library—enhance your read-alouds with sound effects and music to captivate your audience and bring books to life.

---

[4]Jane Doonan, *Looking at Pictures in Picture Books* (New York: Routledge, 2015).
[5]Elaine Moss, "A Certain Particularity: An Interview with Janet and Allan Ahlberg," *Signal* 61 (January 1, 1990): 20.

03 "Game-changer": Reading Aloud with Novel Effect Soundscapes

> Sound is a big part of what makes us human. It's one of the most powerful tools for communication and emotion.
>
> *– Hans Zimmer*

> Music expresses that which cannot be put into words and that which cannot remain silent.
>
> *– Victor Hugo*

Novel Effect soundscapes are created to help foster lifelong readers. With nearly 1,000 soundscapes and counting available on the app, soundscapes enhance stories by adding another layer of enjoyment and context, adding music and highlighting details of illustrations with background sounds and voices as you read, encouraging children to notice and engage more deeply with the story.

Soundscapes transform a reading session into a dynamic, immersive experience that captures children's attention and enhances their comprehension—without diminishing the teacher's role. By layering sound effects and music corresponding to the story, we address additional sensory needs, making the narrative more concrete and engaging for young listeners—and we hear from teachers that they make stories more accessible for children who are multilingual, hearing impaired, or neurodiverse. These auditory cues help children better understand the emotions and actions in the story, supporting comprehension and keeping them engaged from start to finish.

We think of a soundscape as a third pillar, alongside the words and illustrations of a book, working together to bring a story to vivid life. Soundscapes help readers and listeners notice subtleties in illustrations, emotions not conveyed in the text, and other details that enrich a story and deepen the reader's connection to its characters.

But the reader is always in the driver's seat. Novel Effect soundscapes respond to your voice in real-time, with the app listening for cues and playing custom music and sounds that match the story's emotions and actions. Our composers and sound designers thoughtfully create these elements to reflect the author's and illustrator's intentions, ensuring each page comes alive with appropriate audio enhancements.

With the app running on a phone hidden from the children's view, there is no screen involved, eliminating the typical technology distraction. This is a huge point. You want children to be focused on the reader and the story, not the tech or the screen. Tech used correctly blends seamlessly into the real world and unfolds as if magic.

Everyone reads at different speeds, pauses at different points, and internally reflects at different junctures in the story. How then can you create a system that makes it feel magical for everyone? Speech recognition is the key that unlocks the real-time and dynamic nature of a Novel Effect soundscape. It allows the soundscape to follow the reader's pace, ensuring the reading experience remains seamless and natural whatever your cadence or style. It's like being a singer with a live band that adjusts to the singer's pace, rather than the singer keeping up with the music.

Soundscapes are meticulously designed to accommodate various levels of reading fluency, so young readers, should they want to try it for themselves, won't feel discouraged if they miss or mispronounce a word. This adaptability extends to different accents, providing an inclusive and supportive environment for all readers.

In this chapter, we'll describe the elements of soundscapes and how they can enhance your read-aloud sessions, enriching the storytelling experience for both reader and listener.

Elements of a Soundscape

At Novel Effect, we aim for every soundscape to captivate listeners by dynamically responding to the reader with imaginative choices that enhance the narrative. Soundscape designers strive to amplify and enrich the emotions crafted by the author and illustrator, deepening the story's impact.

Creating a soundscape involves a blend of music composition, sound design, sound effects editing, interaction design, voiceover scripting, and voice acting. These elements enrich the characters, drama, tone, theme, and setting of the story, creating a more engaging and dynamic reading experience.

Each soundscape is comprised of various elements that add an extra dimension to a story. Each of these elements—described in the following sections—helps the reader engage with the story. It makes them sit up and pay particular attention to what's happening in the story. What will they hear next? What will they feel as the story continues? What new place will they get to travel to?

Interactive Music

Interactive music included in soundscapes makes the listener feel a particular emotion, transports them to the setting, and reflects the overall tone of the book. While reading *Tap the Magic Tree*, for example, the music makes listeners feel as if something wonderful will happen after they complete an action. It builds anticipation, which keeps the reader anxious for more.

Another example is *Creepy Carrots*: The music creates a sense of fear and anticipation. It incorporates elements of horror to set the creepy tone, and at key moments, illustrates the fear Jasper is experiencing.

Ambiance

Together with the music, we layer ambiance to set the background of the story. From gentle crickets in a nighttime scene to the sounds of a busy city sidewalk hustling and bustling to the chitter-chatter of students before the bell rings, ambiance is important to feel the realism of the soundscape and the story.

Theme

Using music, soundscape designers select instruments, pitch, and pace that help illustrate the story's theme. In *Big* by Vashti Harrison, the music helps readers feel the ways in which the girl is crushed by perpetual comments about her size and then has a slight shift as she grows into herself and comes to love herself.

Sound Effects

Sound effects bring meaning to unknown words, places, or situations. *The Book with No Pictures*, for example, includes interactive sound effects like record scratches, crying, and other engaging sounds that bring meaning to the utterly preposterous situation. This soundscape amplifies the fun and silliness of this book. In other books, sound effects draw readers into the illustrations.

Character Reactions

Character reactions are a lot of fun when using Novel Effect. While reading *This Book Just Ate My Dog*, you understand the main character's excitement, confusion, anger, and urgency every time you hear her voice in the soundscape. Listeners of this soundscape get to experience firsthand a range of emotions. Character reactions also offer an opportunity to bring down the house with funny jokes and humor, as well as deeply connect to characters and elicit compassion and empathy from readers.

Empathy for Characters and Mood

Each soundscape is created with the same level of thought, care, empathy, and expertise—and, crucially, a genuine love and appreciation for children's literature.

Novel Effect soundscape designer Eric Lagergren's work on *My Shadow Is Pink* is a great example of this. The story, which encourages discussions about individuality and acceptance, has an upbeat and interactive soundscape that makes the learning experience fun and positive.

The main character is a young boy with a bright pink shadow that loves sparkles and dresses, but he hides this side of himself because his family has strong blue shadows. Lagergren says he felt a deep connection to the book right from the start. "*My Shadow Is Pink* struck such an emotional, personal chord with me during the first read through. I saw myself in the book's protagonist," he shares.

Using his own experiences, Lagergren created music to match the boy's gentle and playful nature. He chose a flute and celesta to play a "playfully gentle waltz" that represents the boy's love for dresses. These instruments help capture the light and whimsical essence of the boy's shadow.

The soundscape also portrays the boy's father, who has a gruff exterior. To reflect this, Lagergren used a bassoon to create a theme that is "march-like and rough in timbre." This musical contrast shows the struggles and disconnect between the father and son.

As the story unfolds and the father and son start to connect, their musical themes also come together. "The dad's theme morphs into a waltz that plays off of the boy's theme, while the boy's theme appears at an upbeat tempo in 4/4 time," Lagergren explains. This blending of music symbolizes the characters' journey toward understanding and accepting each other.

Through these careful choices, Lagergren's soundscape shows how the characters can keep their individuality while appreciating what makes each other special. This thoughtful creation enhances the story and supports its message of individuality and acceptance.

Making Soundscapes Playful

Because each soundscape is carefully designed for each individual book, a lot of thought goes into the decisions our designers make when ensuring the result truly adds a new dimension to transform the read aloud experience. To illustrate this, we'll share the story of how one of our designers, Kyler Wilkins, approached the creation of the interactive elements and creative sound design for the book *Mix It Up*.

Drawn to the book's unique, genre-less nature, Wilkins saw an opportunity for an a cappella soundscape, recognizing its experimental potential. "A cappella is genre-less. It's an experiment. I can play with sounds . . . add in different singing ideas," Wilkins explains.

Playfulness was key in Wilkins's design. He utilized music to infuse fun into the reading experience, aligning with the book's interactive prompts. For instance, the book instructs readers to press the pages together, building anticipation for what comes next. Reflecting on this, Wilkins noted, "The hardest thing was knowing where to go next from a transition to a new phase. How do you convey experimentation?" His solution was to craft soundscapes that dynamically respond to these interactive moments.

Listeners will notice that some songs include lyrics that directly explain what's happening, such as "Yellow, blue, you know what I mean? Yellow and blue, we shake and make green." In other moments, the soundscape subtly guides readers through the story. For example, when the book instructs readers to tilt the page, Wilkins adds a chorus of voices singing "tiiiiillllt" in layers, creating an engaging auditory cue.

Wilkins also incorporates layers of gospel influences into the soundscape when all the colors appear, enhancing the book's vibrant moments. This layering not only adds depth but also mirrors the book's playful and experimental spirit.

The soundscape empowers readers by staying true to the book's interactive nature. Wilkins designed it to balance between filling the space and inviting the reader to contribute. Early on, Wilkins sings the color names, but as the reading progresses, he omits them, encouraging readers to sing or say the colors themselves.

To keep listeners engaged, Wilkins used a steady beatboxing rhythm as a base layer, maintaining a tempo that's lively yet not rushed. Playful mouth pops, boops, and vocal riffs further invite readers to be silly and creative. This thoughtful composition ensures that the soundscape enhances the book's energy and supports readers in taking control of the story, making the reading experience both immersive and interactive.

Incorporating Soundscapes in Your Read-Aloud

Using a soundscape during a read-aloud is as simple as choosing a book, finding its corresponding soundscape on the Novel Effect app, and tapping play when you're ready to begin. Then you can put the phone aside and hold the attention of your audience.

It is not an audiobook; it is you, the teacher or parent, reading as you would during your storytime to your students or your child on your lap. This approach adds music and sound effects that follow your voice, ensuring you remain the primary focus and maintain the connection with the children and the book.

The interactive nature of soundscapes is a key feature. The technology listens for where the reader is in the book and responds with custom music and sounds. Natural pauses in the teacher's reading are filled with appropriate sound effects, enhancing the storytelling experience by directly responding to the text being read.

Drawing Out Details Not in the Text

When designing soundscapes, careful attention is given to the illustrations, which are studied closely to ensure they align with the auditory elements, enhancing the visual and emotional experience for students. This detailed consideration can also reveal new insights into familiar books, helping teachers and children notice aspects they might not have observed before. This deeper engagement can lead to more insightful discussions and a richer reading experience for both students and educators.

For example, in the book *If I Built a School*, our director of production drew attention to a character—a very expressive-looking dog—in the background of this story taking place in a futuristic school. Even though the dog isn't mentioned in the text, he's there in the illustrations, reacting to the new technology. His ears perk up, and his tail wags as he playfully nips at the hovering desks.

The sound effects bring the dog's presence to life, adding a layer of detail that enriches the story and makes the illustrations more engaging. This subtle addition helps highlight the small details that might otherwise go unnoticed, enhancing the overall reading experience.

Interactive Reading

Reading aloud with a soundscape also offers many opportunities for interaction with children as you read. Here are just a few ideas:

- Tell students to listen for particular sound effects and have them complete a specific action. For example, when they hear the sound of the wind, they get up to sway and gently blow a breeze.
- Before reading, ask them to predict what sounds, characters, or music they think they'll hear. Then have them pop up and say, "Nailed it!" when their predictions come true.
- After listening to the soundscape, let students critique it. What did they like and what did they wish had been included?
- Play a game of "who did it better." Invite students to recreate a part of the soundscape and vote on who did it better; the students or the soundscape designer.
- When students hear a word and then act it out, they understand that the print said something that has a meaning behind it.

Interacting with students in this way as you read keeps them engaged and improves comprehension by encouraging a more active and participatory learning environment. Soundscapes are an excellent tool for facilitating this interaction, providing auditory cues and background sounds that draw students into the story. This multisensory approach helps students better understand and retain the material, making the reading experience more enjoyable and educational.

Rediscovering the Magic: How Soundscapes Revitalize Beloved Stories

One of the best parts of our journey so far is getting to hear all the wonderful stories of the lives we've been privileged to impact. Melinda Louvier, a librarian from Pearland, Texas, reached out one day to share her story that is a testament to the lasting impact read-alouds can have not only on your kids, but on you. In her own words, here's her story.

I want to share something very personal with you all. My all-time favorite book, no matter how old I get, will always be *Where the Wild Things Are* by Maurice Sendak. I was thrilled to see it among the books you've created soundscapes for! It's the book I've used to demo your app to anyone who will stand still for five minutes.

My four kids are all grown now—aged 30, 28, 25, and 20—but when they were little, I read that book to them multiple times a day until we all had it memorized. I have an old videotape of my oldest, at 18 months, turning the pages and reciting the words exactly as they appeared—not because she was reading, but because she knew them by heart. When my kids asked for the story in the car, I'd recite it from memory while driving since I was a single mom and couldn't read while driving.

I must have bought about twenty copies of that book over the years, both for my classrooms when I taught and for my own children. They loved each copy to pieces—getting oatmeal on the pages, chewing the corners, or dropping it in the toilet during potty training. I'd always buy another copy because that book was a constant in their lives. Every book shower I've been to, I've gifted *Where the Wild Things Are*, hoping every kid grows up loving it as much as I do.

This past weekend, I asked my youngest—my twenty-year-old son—if he had five minutes for me to show him something. I don't have a copy of the book anymore, so I turned on my Bluetooth speaker, launched the app, and recited *Where the Wild Things Are* from memory, letting the soundscape play. The look on his face was pure magic! Even at twenty, he had tears in his eyes and was astonished. Hearing the theme music and the wild things roar like he always imagined was priceless. I wished the book was longer so I could stretch out the moment.

When it ended, he walked around the living room, swinging his arms and taking deep breaths. I asked what was wrong, and he said, "Not a single thing, mama. I just wasn't prepared for that!" I apologized for not giving him a heads-up, but he said, "No, it was perfect. It was nice to feel that again!"

I'm sitting at work bawling as I type this, but I want to thank you from the bottom of my heart for what you've done for children everywhere, and especially for that five minutes of magic at my house last weekend. I will never forget it as long as I live.

Up Next . . .

Novel Effect soundscapes have been shown to make reading more enjoyable, interactive, and accessible, helping children develop a love of reading. Our diverse and ever-growing library of sound-scapes, organized by themes and genres, provides not only the perfect soundscape for each book but also corresponding activities to continue the learning and enjoyment after the read-aloud is complete.

Our talented, dedicated composers, musicians, sound designers, writers, and voice actors ensure that each soundscape features a wide array of effects. These sounds are sometimes created digitally with synthesizers, while at other times, sound designers venture outdoors or into local environments with portable field recorders and microphones to capture authentic sounds like a train's whistle, a flowing brook, or the calls of wildlife. Each soundscape succeeds in adding nuance, depth, and emotion to bring a story to life.

All of this work aims to guide and support children on their path to literacy, which we will discuss in the next chapter. Our goal is to help children develop the reading skills they need while fostering a lifelong enjoyment of reading.

Your Reading Brain: The Foundations of Literacy

Reading is a multifaceted skill that our brains have learned to master over millennia. It's not something we're born knowing how to do; it requires careful cultivation and practice from an early age. Astonishingly, what took our brains millennia to develop, we now expect our children to learn in just a few years!

Our goal with Novel Effect is to support children in their literacy journey. We do this by making reading fun and community-focused, but we also have a deep understanding of the science of learning to read. The activities we design for each story in our library (you'll find many examples in Part II) have been carefully created by our team of teachers and librarians to help support children's development of reading skills.

Becoming literate is the cornerstone of lifelong learning, and requires complex interplay of skills that begins long before a child first opens a book. Understanding and nurturing these building blocks—phonemic awareness, phonics, vocabulary, fluency, and comprehension—form the bedrock of a child's ability to decode, understand, and, we hope, develop a love for the written word.

But while phonics instruction remains crucial for developing decoding skills, it must be complemented by activities that promote comprehension, meaning-making, and a love of reading. On this point, research is clear and undisputed: A child's best path to becoming an eager, enthusiastic reader—even before fully "cracking the code" or indeed even entering the classroom—is to be read to, and to engage in other activities that involve "literacy."

As neuropsychologist and child development expert Maryanne Wolf writes in her book *Proust and the Squid: The Story and Science of the Reading Brain*: "The emergent pre-reader sits on 'beloved laps,' samples and learns from a full range of multiple sounds, words, concepts, images, stories, exposure to print, literacy materials, and just plain talk during the first five years of life. The major insight in this period is that reading never just happens to anyone. Emerging reading arises out of years of perceptions, increasing conceptual and social development, and cumulative exposures to oral and written language."[1]

In this chapter, we will explore how literacy development begins at birth and progresses from infancy to school age. We'll examine how the brain navigates through these stages, from recognizing letters and sounds early on to understanding complex texts late—and, of course, we'll highlight how reading aloud with a child is so valuable in their pursuit of literacy learning. But first, let's delve into how our brains adapted to the incredible skill in the first place.

How Our Brains Adapted for Reading

Reading is a fascinating ability that the human brain has adapted for over time—it's not "hardwired" into our brains in the same way as spoken language or basic motor skills. Reading and writing

---

[1] Maryanne Wolf, *Proust and the Squid: The Story and Science of the Reading Brain* (New York: HarperCollins, 2007).

are *learned* skills that require deliberate instruction and practice. Instead, reading is a cultural and cognitive ability that relies on our brain's remarkable flexibility and capacity for learning. Our brains have to adapt to learn to read—specifically in regions like the visual cortex and language centers.

Think about that: The visual cortex, originally specialized for processing basic visual information, has been repurposed over evolutionary time to recognize and interpret written symbols! It shows just how flexible our brains are, able to reorganize and tackle new challenges like interpreting written language.

From its humble beginnings as a cultural invention—such as ancient pictograms and hieroglyphs—reading has evolved into a cornerstone of human communication and knowledge dissemination. This transformation underscores not only the plasticity of the human brain but also its ability to evolve alongside societal changes and technological advancements in writing systems.

As we continue to study the neuroscience of reading, we deepen our understanding of how these cognitive processes unfold and adapt across different individuals and cultures. While reading may not be instinctual, our brains are uniquely equipped to develop the ability.

Now, let's have a look at the stages of literacy and how the brain—and the budding reader—develop along the way. Understanding how our brains adapt for reading is crucial as we explore the stages of literacy development—from recognizing letters to comprehending complex texts, each stage building upon the neurological foundations of our reading brains.

Stages of Literacy

Many scholars and educators have put forward various models to explain how children learn to read (see the sidebar "Looking at Various Reading Stage Models," for some examples). While these models can differ in their details, they generally come together around a common framework of five distinct stages, which we have outlined in Table 4-1.

Table 4-1 The Five Stages of Literacy

Stage 1: Pre-emergent/ Emergent	Ages 0–4	Skills: • Print awareness • Oral language development • Phonemic awareness • Letter recognition • Early writing (such as drawing, "scribbling")
Stage 2: Early reading	Ages 5–7	Skills: • Phonics • Sight words • Reading comprehension • Reading fluency • Vocabulary development • Early writing (such as understanding writing conventions, expressing ideas)
Stage 3: Transitional reading	Ages 7–9	Skills: • Reading fluency • Comprehension strategies (such as visualizing or metacognition) • Expanding vocabulary • Varied text genres (fiction, nonfiction) • Reading for different purposes • Writing development
Stage 4: Intermediate reading	Ages 9–12	Skills: • Reading comprehension • Critical thinking • Text analysis • Diverse reading materials • Reading stamina • Writing skills

(Continued)

Table 4-1   (Continued)

Stage 5: Advanced reading	Ages 12+	Skills: • Deep comprehension (e.g. thinking beyond the text, making connections, changing perspectives) • Critical analysis • Synthesis and evaluation • Advanced vocabulary • Reading for various purposes • Advanced writing skills

The stages outline and describe how reading skills progress—from building foundational basics to achieving advanced comprehension. Each development stage builds on the previous one, which is why early literacy is so crucial, as a child cannot move on to the next stage before achieving the competencies of the first.

The stages of literacy development presented here are widely recognized in the field of literacy education, representing a progression of skills from early childhood through adolescence. They reflect a consensus on the typical milestones in reading and writing acquisition.

Interesting to note: Five-year-olds have significant developmental shifts at age five and five and a half. It's pretty cool how they change around the half birthday!

Looking at Various Reading Stage Models

The following are examples of various models that offer different perspectives on the progression of literacy skills, each emphasizing various aspects of cognitive and linguistic development in relation to reading.

Four-Stage Model (Marie Clay): Marie Clay, a renowned educational psychologist, proposed a four-stage model that focuses on early emergent literacy, basic reading skills, fluent reading, and reading for learning.

Six-Stage Model (Jerry Johns): Jerry Johns, an influential figure in literacy education, developed a six-stage model that includes emergent literacy, initial reading and decoding, confirmation and fluency, reading to learn, multiple viewpoints, and construction and reconstruction.

Three-Stage Model (Betty Hart and Todd R. Risley): Betty Hart and Todd R. Risley's research on early language development outlines a three-stage model: emergent literacy, early reading skills, and fluent reading.

Seven-Stage Model (David R. Olson and Nancy Torrance): David R. Olson and Nancy Torrance proposed a seven-stage model that delineates literacy development into stages such as early phonological awareness, decoding, fluency, vocabulary growth, comprehension, reading for learning, and critical reading.

The Pre-emergent Stage: The Infant Brain

Let's start at the very beginning: the infant brain. Although cultivating literacy skills may be the last thing one considers when holding a newborn baby, the learning is already starting.

In their book *Emergent Literacy*, William H. Teale and Elizabeth Sulzby, who coined the phrase, write: "Emergent literacy is concerned with the earliest phases of literacy development, the period between birth and the time when children read and write conventionally. The term emergent literacy signals a belief that, in a literate society, young children–even one- and two-year-olds–are in the process of becoming literate."[2]

It may sound odd to say learning begins in infancy, but science supports this. Experts encourage talking with and reading to babies from the very beginning–even if they cannot understand you, it increases the communication bond and sets the stage for later comprehension. Over time, hearing these words repeatedly will help them begin to understand their meaning.

---

[2]William H. Teale and Elizabeth Sulzby, *Emergent Literacy* (Baltimore: Paul H. Brookes Publishing Co., 1986).

The Emergent Literacy Stage

Emergent readers are typically children in the age range of birth to around six years old. This period is crucial for the development of foundational literacy skills, as shown in Table 4-1. Here is a more detailed breakdown:

Learning letters of the alphabet: This is the stage where young children, even toddlers, begin to identify the letters, names, and sounds of the alphabet.

Print concepts: The understanding that printing letters and words have meaning in language.

Oral language development: This is a key step toward reading and writing! It is the stage where children begin to listen and respond in speech.

Decoding: Recognizing sounds and understanding how they form words, with phonemic awareness being a critical component often linked to decoding skills.

Fluency: The ability to read smoothly with understanding and comprehension, which is crucial for literacy development.

Vocabulary: Learning new words and associating them with objects or ideas, starting with letter identification and understanding the significance of letters when combined.

Sentence Structure and Cohesion: Developing the ability to construct coherent sentences, first through spoken language and later in writing and reading.

Experience and Reasoning: Using personal experiences and background knowledge to create and understand stories, whether they are imagined or derived from reading material.

Working Memory and Attention: Developing executive functions that enable children to complete complex tasks, such as matching and identifying elements of a book or story, and building on these skills as they grow.

It is important, at all stages, to promote a growth mindset around reading and writing so children understand that these skills can be developed with effort and practice.

Praising effort rather than innate ability encourages children to persist through challenges and view mistakes as learning opportunities. This mindset fosters resilience and a positive attitude toward literacy learning.

Activities That Support Literacy Development

Now that we've outlined the stages of literacy development, let's turn our attention to practical strategies that foster early literacy skills from birth. These activities lay the groundwork for children to become successful readers and writers.

Research strongly supports literacy is enhanced by engaging in activities with parents that may not on the surface "look" like literacy—when children engage in real-world, purposeful activities that involve a degree of "literacy." This can include activities like mimicking making grocery lists or pretending to talk on the phone.

By integrating the following foundational activities into daily routines, parents and educators can set the stage for a lifetime of literacy and learning. Read-alouds, in particular, serve as a powerful tool to bring these elements together, creating a rich tapestry of language and learning that benefits every child.

Playing

Engaging in play helps children learn new vocabulary and gives them a head start in reading. This underscores the importance of allowing children ample time for play. However, this is increasingly challenged as recess periods are shortened in favor of more "academic" activities.

Studies indicate that when children engage in imaginative play that mirrors real-life situations—such as setting up a pretend hardware store or playing teacher with their stuffed animals—they enhance and expand their vocabulary. When children play together, this type of self-directed play encourages them to understand and use language creatively, laying a strong foundation for reading skills. Even when adults join in to guide the play or introduce new games, children gain valuable opportunities to develop their literacy skills in a fun and creative way.

Having props and writing materials available also encourages literacy learning—for example, putting a mini library in a playroom or including notebooks and pens in a pretend office setup. These familiar items inspire kids to integrate reading and writing into their play, making literacy a natural part of their activities. This makes the process of learning to read and write a seamless and enjoyable part of their playtime.

Singing

Singing is a wonderful activity for emergent readers—and actually, for anyone. Its many perks include developing vocabulary in context, which helps them better understand how to use words correctly in their own conversations or writings. The repetition reinforces the meaning and helps them expand their vocabulary. It has also been shown to improve speech and pronunciation and develop phonemic awareness and auditory discrimination. Also, following a beat or copying a rhythm later supports an ability to recognize and connect spelling patterns. Plus it's fun.

Beyond these skills, singing can help children in their emotional development as well as cognitive skills, with songs that involve counting, learning opposites, or sequencing. Social skills, listening skills, improved memory—a few rounds of "The Wheels on the Bus" brings these benefits and more.

Talking

This may seem obvious, that talking with your students expands their vocabulary. But there are strategies you can apply so students gets the most out of these interactions. One such strategy shown to be effective is extending a child's own sentences in your response. So, for example, if a student says, "I saw a dog," you can ask, "Was it a big brown dog or a small white one?"

In the same way that adults make mistakes when learning a second (or indeed third) language, children learn by hearing words over and over, in meaningful context. Sometimes, it's a matter of trial and error until you get it right.

Rephrasing, rather than correcting, a child when they make mistakes helps them learn without feeling embarrassed, which discourages them from taking "language risks" (trying on new words or expressions) in the future. For example, children developing literacy skills may make a mistake conjugating an irregular verb—which is actually a smart mistake, as they are applying a standard rule! So if they say, "I go'ed to the park," you can say, "Oh, you went to the park yesterday?"

Drawing

Drawing and scribbling is often considered the first step to writing because it helps children develop essential skills directly related to writing. It aids in fine motor skills development, improving dexterity and coordination, and enhances hand-eye coordination. Drawing also improves visual and spatial awareness by familiarizing children with shapes and lines, the building blocks of letters and numbers, and teaching them spatial organization, crucial for letter placement and word spacing.

In addition, it fosters symbolic thinking, allowing children to understand that objects, people, and ideas can be represented through symbols, which is foundational for grasping that letters and words represent sounds and meanings, and helps develop cognitive skills, such as pattern recognition and problem-solving, important for understanding language structure and constructing sentences.

Buddy Reading

Buddy reading can make reading more engaging and enjoyable, especially for reluctant readers. With buddy reading, children are paired together to read a book, making it both a social activity and one that supports learning. Partners take turns reading passages aloud to each other, which helps improve their reading fluency, punctuation, and confidence. It also improves comprehension, as partners discuss the story during and after shared reading. They can ask each other questions, summarize what they've read, and discuss how they feel about the story.

Writing

Writing connects spoken and written language. Helping children learn to write and practice writing can be both fun and educational (we discuss developing writing skills in more detail in Chapter 5).

There are several activities you can encourage, such as providing worksheets with dotted letters for them to trace, using a whiteboard or magnetic letters to help them practice letters and words, or encourage them to write their own stories, perhaps with the help of a prompt.

Practicing writing by copying a sentence from a favorite book or labeling objects with sticky notes also provides excellent writing experience. Tasks like writing to-do lists or thank-you notes or labeling objects using sticky notes all provide opportunities to practice and improve writing skills. Additionally, children who read or are read to a lot, exposed to a range of genres, learn how to write from repeated exposure to writing experts.

Creating a Print-Rich Environment

Creating a print-rich environment in the classroom is so important we are giving it its own section in this chapter. Research has supported that simply being around books sets children up for later academic success.

For example, a comprehensive study drawing on data from thirty-one countries, including the United States and Canada, revealed that those who grew up with home libraries exhibit superior reading comprehension and enhanced mathematical abilities as adults.

Led by Joanna Sikora, a senior sociology lecturer at Australian National University, the research team identified 80 books as a pivotal number: Study participants who had approximately

80 books in their homes showed average literacy levels. In contrast, those from homes with fewer than 80 books generally had below-average literacy. Literacy levels continued to improve with the number of books up to 350, beyond which the effect plateaued.

But before you rush out to buy hundreds of books, here are some simple tips for creating a print-rich environment in the classroom:

- **Create a reading corner.** Having a comfortable, quiet place to read is a great way to encourage children to want to read. And think beyond the book: To make it attractive, you can also provide other types of reading materials, including comics, magazines, newspapers, and reference books like atlases and dictionaries.
- **Display children's work.** Have children create artwork or posters that are text-rich and display them around the classroom. Take time to read aloud the text and engage with the children about it.
- **Post morning routines.** Displaying information about the schedule for the day, the times in which certain activities will take place, who has a birthday, what the date and season is—anything that relates to the child's experience in the world—is a great way to engage them in the print around them.

Theories and Approaches of Teaching Reading in School

Having explored effective activities for nurturing literacy skills, it's essential to understand the theories and approaches guiding how we teach reading in schools. Balancing practical activities with evidence-based instructional methods ensures a holistic approach to literacy education.

Educators have been working to identify the most effective strategy for teaching reading to children for decades, and there continues to be a search for the ideal approach. The following sections outline some of the methods that have been embraced before being contested.

Phonics-Based Approach

Phonics instruction has long been regarded as a crucial component of early reading development. This approach focuses on teaching children the relationships between letters and sounds, enabling them to decode unfamiliar words by sounding them out. Synthetic phonics, in particular, emphasizes the systematic and sequential teaching of letter-sound correspondences, while analytic phonics encourages children to analyze whole words and their constituent parts.

Advocates of phonics instruction argue that it provides children with strong decoding skills, essential for reading success. Research supports the effectiveness of explicit phonics instruction in improving early reading achievement, especially for struggling readers. However, critics caution that a strict focus on phonics may overlook the importance of comprehension and meaning-making in reading. Moreover, some argue that phonics instruction can be dry and fail to engage children's interest in reading.

Whole Language Approach

In contrast to phonics-based instruction, the whole language approach prioritizes reading for meaning and comprehension. Children are encouraged to recognize whole words and use context cues to understand the text. Whole language instruction integrates reading, writing, speaking, and listening, fostering a holistic approach to language development.

Proponents of the whole language approach argue that it promotes a love of reading and a deeper understanding of texts. By emphasizing comprehension and meaning-making, whole language instruction aims to create lifelong readers who engage with texts critically and analytically. However, critics contend that without explicit phonics instruction, children may struggle with decoding unfamiliar words, leading to difficulties in reading fluency and comprehension.

Balanced Literacy Approach

Recognizing the strengths and limitations of both phonics-based and whole language approaches, many educators advocate for a balanced literacy approach. This approach seeks to integrate explicit phonics instruction with activities that promote reading for meaning and enjoyment. Balanced literacy programs often include guided reading, read-alouds, shared reading, and opportunities for independent reading and writing.

Proponents of balanced literacy argue that it provides a comprehensive approach to reading instruction, addressing both decoding skills and comprehension. By combining the strengths of phonics and whole language, balanced literacy programs aim to meet the diverse needs of students and create lifelong readers. However, critics caution that without clear guidelines and effective implementation, balanced literacy programs may become uneven mixes that fail to effectively teach either decoding or comprehension skills.

The Science of Reading

The "Science of Reading" movement is an educational initiative that emphasizes evidence-based approaches to teaching reading, grounded in cognitive science and neuroscience research. It highlights the importance of systematic, explicit phonics instruction as foundational for reading proficiency. This approach poses that teaching children to decode words by understanding sound-letter relationships (phonemic awareness) is essential, especially in early education.

The movement contrasts with methods that focus more on whole language approaches or less structured phonics, which emphasize learning to read through exposure to text and context-based guessing. Supporters of the Science of Reading stress that a phonics-based approach is more effective, particularly for struggling readers, as it aligns with how the brain processes written language.

Interview with Christi Unker

Novel Effect: Hi Christi! We're excited to talk with you about your work with Novel Effect. Can you tell us how you ended up at the Kentucky School for the Blind?

I've been at the Kentucky School for the Blind for about seven years and have been a librarian for twenty-five. Before this, I worked as an elementary, middle, and high school librarian. Someone posted on our state listserv that there was an opening at the School for the Blind. I was intrigued by the challenge. I had a Training and Development and Library Science degree, but I also had to get a Master's in Visual Impairments. We learn about visual impairments, how to read Braille, and adapt materials for our students.

What age range do you work with at the Kentucky School for the Blind?

We start with kindergarten and go up to age twenty-one. There's a separate preschool for children with visual impairments in our state. About 40 percent of our kids live on campus because they live too far away to be transported daily. If they live within an hour and a half, they are bused in, but if they're further out, they live in our dorm. We never have snow days because our kids are always here!

Do you use Novel Effect with all your students?

I primarily use it with elementary students but have also used it with middle school kids. I read aloud to them, but they love it when I set out twin vision Braille books and preload the iPads with the corresponding soundscapes. The library is big, so I put them in corners of the room to practice reading. They're motivated by the sounds.

What are twin vision books?

Each state has a regional library that provides materials for the visually impaired. Ours is the Kentucky Talking Book Library. They send us free copies of elementary books in Braille. Twin vision books have an overlay with Braille text alongside print text, which helps parents who don't know Braille read with their kids. For middle school books, it switches to all Braille with no pictures or print.

Are you able to use Novel Effect book activities with your students?

Yes! We have an embosser, a printer that produces Braille instead of print. I can create tactile images with it. For example, I can emboss a dotted outline of a bear that students can feel. Novel Effect's activity emails give me great ideas to modify for my kids.

What challenges has Novel Effect helped solve?

Before Novel Effect, I used to queue up sounds manually, like when I read *The Polar Express*. Now, the app does it for me. It's especially helpful for students reluctant to read. They're more likely to pick up Braille books because they know they'll hear sounds as a reward. It motivates them to practice reading skills independently.

What's your favorite part about the app as an educator?

I love seeing what sounds you come up with! I was excited to find *The Three Billy Goats Gruff* in your library. The sounds enhance the story so well.

Do you and your students have any favorite books to read with Novel Effect?

Zin! Zin! Zin! A Violin by Lloyd Moss and *Dragons Love Tacos* by Adam Rubin are our favorites. The kids love them!

Up Next . . .

This chapter covered a lot of ground in activities and practices that support early literacy skills in children, even before they start school. Literacy begins at birth and stems and grows through interactions with others and the world. It's never too early to start supporting a child's literacy journey.

Novel Effect works to support this journey by making reading fun, but we understand the science behind developing as readers. In the next chapter, we'll look at how children can be encouraged to share their own stories as budding writers.

05 Developing Young Writers and Storytellers

I write entirely to find out what I'm thinking, what I'm looking at, what I see and what it means. What I want and what I fear.

– Joan Didion

You have to write the book that wants to be written. And if the book will be too difficult for grown-ups, then you write it for children.

– Madeleine L'Engle

Our goal at Novel Effect is to help children cultivate a love of reading by offering them a read-aloud experience that is engaging, exciting, and pulls them into the story. But we also want to encourage children to become young writers, to share their own ideas and imaginations through the age-old art of storytelling.

Storytelling captivates young minds, immersing them in narrative structures and sparking their imaginations. When children engage in stories through tools like Novel Effect, where sound effects and interactive elements serve to engage readers and increase comprehension of and connection to a story, they are not only entertained but also inspired to become storytellers themselves.

Sharing ideas and experiences in stories is a fundamental aspect of human experience, and its impact on children is profound. From the earliest days, children are drawn to the magic of stories, intrigued by the adventures and characters that exist and reveal themselves in the pages of a book. Reading to children helps them understand that books are gateways to these wonderful stories, as well as rich sources of information. This early exposure is crucial for their development, both cognitively and socially.

Storytelling also fosters empathy and emotional intelligence by introducing children to different perspectives and experiences. As they connect with characters and their journeys, children learn to express their thoughts and feelings more effectively, both verbally and in writing. This emotional engagement with stories encourages children to explore their own ideas and experiences through writing, creating a pathway for self-expression and communication.

Developmentally, storytelling aids in language acquisition and literacy skills. When children listen to stories, they expand their vocabulary, grasp the nuances of language, and learn to structure their thoughts coherently. They learn to predict what will happen next and to express why they think so. These foundational skills are essential as they begin to articulate their own ideas.

Socially, stories foster empathy and understanding. By encountering diverse characters and scenarios, children learn to see the world from different perspectives, cultivating emotional intelligence and a sense of connection to others. And in doing so, they can begin to see what is unique in their own lives—as well as what similarities exist between their experiences and those they read about.

Moreover, storytelling ignites a child's imagination, encouraging them to become creators of their own narratives. Pam Allyn beautifully captures this progression: "Reading is like breathing in, writing is like breathing out."[1] Through stories, children inhale the richness of language and ideas, and through writing, they exhale their creativity and thoughts.

This desire to share their thoughts and stories often begins in simple forms—through scribbling, drawing, or making up tales. These early attempts are significant milestones. By nurturing this

---

[1]Pam Allyn, "Reading Is Like Breathing In; Writing Is Like Breathing Out," *Literacy Now*, July 16, 2015, https://www.literacyworldwide.org/blog/literacy-now/2015/07/16/reading-is-like-breathing-in-writing-is-like-breathing-out.

storytelling instinct, and encouraging children to be writers of their own stories, we empower children to express themselves and share their unique voices with the world, laying the foundation for a lifetime of literary engagement and creative expression.

In this chapter, we will explore the stages of writing development in young children, from scribbling and drawing to conventional spelling and writing. We will discuss how to create a writing-friendly environment and encourage a love for books and reading. We will also cover strategies to motivate writing, including interactive storytelling and writing through play, as well as activities and exercises to support writing skills.

Connections Between Reading, Storytelling, and Writing

In early childhood education, the connections between reading, storytelling, and writing play a crucial role in language development and literacy skills. Reading aloud to young children not only introduces them to vocabulary and language structures but also sparks their imagination and curiosity.

Through storytelling, whether through books, oral traditions, or interactive activities like those facilitated by Novel Effect, children learn narrative structure, sequencing, and the power of imagination. These experiences lay the foundation for writing skills by familiarizing children with the components of stories–characters, settings, plot–and encouraging them to express their own ideas and experiences through drawing, scribbling, and eventually, emergent writing. The process of reading, storytelling, and writing forms a dynamic cycle that fosters language proficiency, creativity, and a lifelong love for learning.

Storytelling and the Brain

Understanding the neuroscience of storytelling reveals its pivotal role not just in education but in crafting memorable and impactful learning experiences. With practical insights and a customizable template, educators can effectively transform information into compelling narratives that resonate with learners.

Storytelling has a profound impact on how our brains process and retain information. When we hear a story, our brain syncs up with the storyteller's brain. This synchrony activates seven key areas, shown in Figure 5-1.

1. Visual Cortex: Processes colors and shapes.

2. Wernicke's Area: Comprehends language.

3. Motor Cortex: Mimics movements.

4. Auditory Cortex: Processes sounds.

5. Broca's Area: Handles language structure.

6. Olfactory Cortex: Evokes scents.

7. Sensory Cortex and Cerebellum: Enhances sensory understanding.

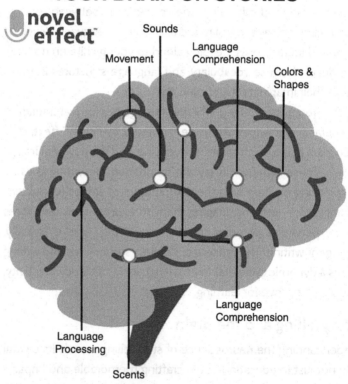

Figure 5-1 The Storyteller's Brain

Source: Savion Ray

In contrast, presenting facts and statistics without story-telling engages only language comprehension areas (Wernicke's Area and Broca's Area; see Figure 5-2). This approach misses out on tapping into the brain's full potential for visualization, empathy, and memory.

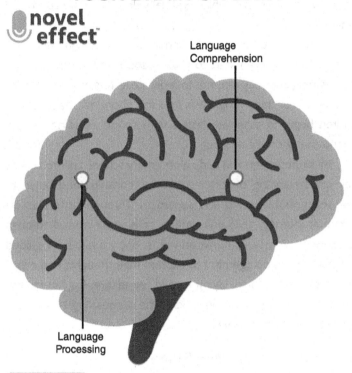

YOUR BRAIN ON DATA

Figure 5-2   Language Comprehension Areas

Source: Savion Ray

Tools like Novel Effect leverage these insights by enhancing educational experiences through immersive narratives, and the writing prompts included in our story-related activities (available on the app for all of our titles, as well as in Part II of this book).

Development of Writing Skills in Young Children

In young children, the development of writing skills progresses through distinct stages, beginning with scribbles and evolving into more structured forms of communication. During the scribbling stage, typically observed in toddlers, children experiment with making marks on paper, which gradually become more controlled and purposeful.

As they enter the pre-phonemic stage, usually around ages three to four, children start to understand that their marks convey meaning and may attempt to replicate letters or symbols they recognize. This stage progresses into the phonemic stage, where children begin to associate letters with sounds, leading to their attempts at phonetic spelling.

By kindergarten and early elementary school, children refine their understanding of letter-sound relationships and begin to write recognizable words and sentences. Throughout this developmental journey, children's writing skills are nurtured through exposure to literacy-rich environments, opportunities for guided practice, and encouragement to express their thoughts and experiences in written form, laying a solid foundation for future academic success. The following looks at the various stages of writing development in more detail.

Scribbling and Drawing Stage

Scribbling is often the earliest form of writing development observed in young children, typically emerging between the ages of twelve to eighteen months. It involves making spontaneous marks on paper or other surfaces using crayons, markers, or pencils. These marks can vary widely in form, from random lines and loops to more purposeful gestures that mimic the movements children see around them. At this stage, scribbles lack conventional shapes or symbols and are primarily exploratory and sensory-driven. Children may also experiment with different tools and techniques, exploring how pressure and movement create different marks.

Scribbling plays a crucial role in laying the foundation for later writing skills. While it may not resemble actual writing, scribbling serves as a precursor to understanding the purpose of written communication. Through scribbling, children begin to develop hand-eye coordination, fine motor skills, and spatial awareness—all essential for controlling writing tools and forming recognizable letters later on.

Scribbling also fosters cognitive development by allowing children to express their thoughts and experiences visually, encouraging creativity and imagination. And it introduces children to the concept that marks on paper can convey meaning, setting the stage for their journey toward more structured forms of writing as they grow and mature.

Recognizing and Replicating Letter Shapes

During the stage of random letters and letter strings, typically observed in children around three to four years old, there is a growing awareness of letter shapes and their symbolic nature. Children begin to recognize individual letters from the alphabet and may show interest in identifying letters in their environment, such as on signs, books, or packaging. They often demonstrate curiosity about letters and their sounds, which is a crucial precursor to understanding phonics and decoding words.

At this stage, children experiment with writing by attempting to replicate letters they recognize. These early attempts may involve irregular letter formations and inconsistent sizing, reflecting their developing fine motor skills and understanding of letter formation rules. While the letters may not be accurately formed or in conventional order, these attempts represent significant progress in understanding the symbolic representation of language.

Children derive satisfaction from their ability to create recognizable shapes and may begin to assign meaning to their written marks, even if they do not yet produce complete words or sentences. This phase marks an important transition from scribbling to more intentional forms of writing as children continue to refine their motor skills and understanding of letter-sound relationships.

"Invented" Spelling and Phonetic Writing

In the stage of invented spelling and phonetic writing, typically seen in children around four to six years old, there is a notable progression in their ability to represent spoken language through written symbols. During this phase, children rely heavily on their understanding of phonetics–the relationship between sounds and letters–to spell words phonetically. They begin to experiment with writing words based on the sounds they hear, rather than adhering strictly to conventional spelling rules. This often results in creative spelling attempts where words are spelled according to their sound patterns, sometimes leading to unconventional but understandable written expressions.

Phonetics plays a crucial role in early writing as children learn to connect sounds to corresponding letters or groups of letters. They apply their growing knowledge of letter-sound relationships to compose words independently, using invented spellings that reflect their evolving phonemic awareness. This process not only supports their emerging literacy skills but also fosters confidence in their ability to communicate through written language.

Invented spelling encourages children to express themselves freely without the constraints of conventional spelling, promoting a sense of ownership and creativity in their writing endeavors. As children progress through this stage, their phonetic writing gradually incorporates more conventional spelling patterns, marking a significant step toward more refined and accurate written communication skills.

Shift to Conventional Spelling

During the phase of conventional spelling, typically emerging around ages six to seven and continuing into early elementary school years, children begin to adopt more standardized and correct spelling patterns. This stage represents a significant leap in their writing development as they move away from relying solely on phonetic approximations and start to internalize conventional spelling rules and patterns. They become increasingly aware of spelling conventions such as silent letters, prefixes, suffixes, and irregular spellings, refining their ability to accurately reproduce words according to accepted norms.

Educators play a crucial role in supporting children's transition to conventional spelling by providing opportunities for guided practice and exposure to varied texts. Activities such as dictation exercises, word games, and reading aloud can help reinforce spelling rules and expand children's vocabulary.

Positive reinforcement and constructive feedback are essential in fostering confidence and motivation as children strive to master correct spelling. By encouraging the use of conventional spelling in a supportive environment, educators help children develop proficiency in written communication, enabling them to express their thoughts and ideas more effectively through written language.

Creating an Environment That Encourages Children to Write

Creating a writing-friendly environment for young children is crucial in fostering their early literacy skills and nurturing a love for writing. This environment encompasses both physical resources and supportive spaces that encourage exploration and creativity in writing.

Using picture books as "anchor texts" and models for good writing is another strategy to encourage children with their own writing, and reading books with Novel Effect further models for children how to add details to make the story more engaging and clear to their reader while also staying true to the intention of the writer.

Access to Writing Materials

Access to a variety of writing materials is essential in stimulating children's interest and engagement in writing activities. Providing a range of tools such as crayons, markers, colored pencils, and different types of pencils allows children to experiment with different writing mediums and develop their fine motor skills. These materials also cater to individual preferences, accommodating children who may find certain tools more comfortable or appealing.

Ensuring an ample supply of paper, notebooks, and other writing surfaces further encourages children to freely express their thoughts and ideas through drawing and writing.

Designated Writing Areas

Designated writing areas within classrooms or home environments create dedicated spaces where children can focus on writing tasks comfortably. These areas should be well-defined, inviting, and organized to promote a sense of ownership and autonomy in writing activities. Setting up writing centers equipped with writing materials, books, and themed prompts or activities can inspire children to engage in various writing experiences independently or with peers. These centers can include cozy reading nooks, accessible shelves stocked with age-appropriate books and writing resources, and display areas to showcase children's completed writing pieces.

Integrating comfortable seating options, such as cushions and bean bags, enhances the appeal of these spaces, making them conducive to extended periods of writing and creative exploration. Establishing a routine where children have dedicated time to visit these writing areas fosters consistency and reinforces the importance of writing as an enjoyable and valuable activity.

Promoting Writing Through Play and Exploration

Young children in particular learn through play and exploration, and integrating writing opportunities into play-based activities enriches their writing experiences. Incorporating writing into dramatic play scenarios, such as setting up a pretend restaurant with menus to write or a post office with letters to address, allows children to naturally integrate writing into their imaginative play. Providing thematic props and materials that encourage writing, such as recipe cards, notepads, and labels, sparks their curiosity and motivation to engage in writing activities as part of their play.

Celebrating and Displaying Children's Writing

Celebrating children's writing achievements reinforces their confidence and pride in their literacy skills. Displaying their completed writing pieces on classroom bulletin boards, creating class books, or organizing writing showcases for families and peers provides opportunities for children to share their work and receive positive feedback. Celebrations can include sharing stories during circle time, inviting guest readers to listen to children's writing, or organizing author celebrations where children read aloud their favorite stories they have written.

Modeling Writing Behavior

Teachers play a significant role in modeling positive attitudes toward writing and demonstrating effective writing practices. Engaging in joint writing activities where teachers write alongside children, such as composing stories together or writing letters, demonstrates the purpose and value of writing in real-world contexts. Modeling writing processes, such as brainstorming ideas, revising drafts, and sharing finished pieces, helps children understand the sequential steps involved in writing and encourages them to develop their writing skills with confidence.

Creating a writing-friendly environment for young children involves intentional planning, supportive resources, and engaging opportunities that nurture their emerging literacy skills. By encouraging a love for writing through accessible materials, inviting spaces, playful integration, celebrations of achievement, and positive role modeling, teachers empower children to explore their creativity, communicate their thoughts effectively, and develop a lifelong appreciation for writing.

Encouraging Young Storytellers Using a Six-Step Outline

Guiding young storytellers to structure their ideas into a narrative can be achieved by breaking a story into manageable steps. We had the privilege of engaging with Educational Consultant LeeAnne Lavender, who shared a transformative six-step outline for turning data and facts into compelling stories.

Inspired by the timeless structure of the hero's journey—a narrative framework embraced by storytellers across the ages–Lavender's process offers a powerful tool for educators and young writers alike. The hero's journey is a common structure, which can be found in the likes of the Star Wars, The Lord of the Rings, and the Harry Potter series.

By implementing these six steps to craft an outline for presenting information, you can convert any lesson or idea into an engaging narrative. This versatile template is ideal for structuring stories in history, English, math–any subject or topic you choose. Let's walk through an example provided by Lavender: the story of Sir Isaac Newton's discovery of gravity.

The following six-step outline can be used to create stories, turning ideas and details into engaging narratives, to help guide children through organizing the elements of a story. They provide a good template for children to begin sharing stories of their own.

Step 1: Determine the Story You Are Sharing

First, identify the big idea you want your audience to remember. What is the learning target or goal you are trying to achieve?

Example: The story of Sir Isaac Newton discovering gravity.

Step 2: Who's Your Hero?

Decide who the main character of your story is. If you are teaching about Sir Isaac Newton, is he the hero of your story? Or is it the concept of gravity itself?

Example: Sir Isaac Newton is the hero of this story!

Step 3: What's the Conflict?

Your hero needs a conflict to overcome. What problem are they facing? What's their biggest challenge?

Example: Sir Isaac Newton is trying to understand why an apple fell from a tree and hit him on the head. Why did it fall instead of floating off into space?

Step 4: The Solution

Describe how the hero resolves the conflict. How do they overcome their problem?

Example: Newton realized that something caused the apple to fall and hit his head. Through extensive research, he determined that the cause was gravity, a force that keeps objects, like people and apples, anchored to the Earth.

Step 5: Transformation

Explain how the solution transforms the lives of the heroes in the story. Be clear and vivid in your description.

Example: By discovering gravity, Sir Isaac Newton realized that Earth wasn't the center of the solar system. This led to the groundbreaking discovery that Earth and the other planets orbit around the Sun!

Step 6: The Emotions Involved

Decide how you want your heroes to feel about their transformation. Should they be happy, sad, excited, or inspired?

Example: Sir Isaac Newton was excited, proud, and happy when he figured out what caused the apple to fall from the tree.

Up Next . . .

We've covered a lot of ground so far, from the power of reading aloud to children, the importance of providing them rich, entertaining, and thought-provoking literature to enjoy, and how young brains learn the cognitive skill of recognizing letters on the page and connecting with their meaning. And, of course, we've described how our carefully crafted soundscapes enhance the read-aloud experience.

In the next chapter, we're going to tie it all together, to walk through the steps of truly rocking your read-aloud sessions with your students, to connect with them, have fun, all the while developing key literacy skills and, most importantly, to set them up for a lifelong enjoyment of reading.

Getting Ready to Rock Your Read Aloud

I have a passion for teaching kids to become readers, to become comfortable with a book, not daunted. Books shouldn't be daunting, they should be funny, exciting and wonderful; and learning to be a reader gives a terrific advantage.

– Roald Dahl

Reading aloud to your children is a gift that will last a lifetime.

– Maya Angelou

Novel Effect was born from our desire to empower teachers to create memorable storytimes. Our goal is to share the joy of reading and ensure that reading together becomes a cherished part of a child's experience. We want to celebrate the wonder of childhood, honor the power of storytime, and enhance the magic of books.

In this chapter, we share what we believe works to make read-aloud sessions truly enjoyable—including strategies for before, during, and after you read. And of course, we explain how to incorporate soundscapes into your read-alouds.

Then, in Part II, you'll find numerous guiding lessons based on a selection from the collection of soundscapes available on the Novel Effect app. Used in tandem, the lessons and sound-scapes are designed to enrich the read-loud experience for both children and adults alike.

Because understanding the events and characters in a book is key to feeling connected to and enjoying a story, we will begin with some general strategies for gauging a child's comprehension as you read, before we walk through the stages of a read-aloud session with Novel Effect.

Comprehension Cognitive Practices for Early Readers

Early readers benefit significantly from engaging in comprehension cognitive practices that enhance their understanding and retention of stories. The following sections discuss some effective comprehension cognitive practices that help early readers develop stronger reading skills, better understand stories, and build a lasting love for reading.

Predicting

Predicting involves making educated guesses about what will happen next in a story based on the text and illustrations. When reading with novel effect, ask students to predict what kind of music they think they'll hear, what sound effects they expect. These practices encourages active engagement and critical thinking.

- Before Reading: Look at the book cover and title, and ask, "What do you think this book will be about?"
- During Reading: Pause at key points and ask, "What do you think will happen next?"
- After Reading: Discuss if their predictions were correct and why.

Summarizing

Summarizing helps children identify the main ideas and key details of a story, aiding in comprehension and retention. Summarizing requires children to synthesize what they read.

- After Reading: Ask the child to state a theme. Ask, "What details from the story help show that theme?"

Visualizing

Visualizing involves creating mental images of the scenes described in the story, which enhances understanding and memory.

- During Reading: Encourage children to imagine what they are hearing. Ask, "What do you see in your mind when I read this part?"
- After Reading: Have them draw a scene from the story or describe it in detail.

Connecting

Making connections between the text and their own experiences helps children relate to the story and enhances comprehension.

- Text-to-Self: Ask, "Does this story remind you of anything that has happened to you?"
- Text-to-Text: Ask, "Does this story remind you of another book we've read?"
- Text-to-World: Ask, "Does this story remind you of anything happening in the world?"

Questioning

Encouraging children to ask and answer questions about the story promotes active reading and critical thinking.

- Before Reading: Ask, "What do you wonder about this book?"
- During Reading: Ask, "Why do you think the character did that?"
- After Reading: Ask, "What was your favorite part?"

Clarifying

Clarifying involves stopping to resolve misunderstandings, ensuring children understand what they are reading.

- During Reading: Pause to explain difficult words or concepts. Ask, "Is there anything you don't understand?"
- After Reading: Discuss any confusing parts and clarify misunderstandings.

Retelling

Retelling the story in their own words helps children understand and remember the sequence of events and details.

- After Reading: Ask the child to retell the story, including as many details as they can.
- Use Props: Use puppets, toys, or drawings to help them retell the story.

Inferring

Inferring involves reading between the lines to understand the underlying meaning or what is not explicitly stated in the text.

- During Reading: Ask, "Why do you think the character feels this way?" or "What do you think the character will do next?" Interpreting the meaning of figurative language and what it says about the character or events.
- After Reading: Discuss any inferred meanings or themes from the story.

Evaluating

Evaluating encourages children to form opinions about what they read, fostering deeper engagement and critical thinking.

- After Reading: Ask, "Did you like the story? Why or why not?" or "What did you think was the most exciting part?"

Monitoring understanding

Monitoring their own understanding and taking steps to correct misunderstandings helps children become more independent readers.

- During Reading: Encourage children to recognize when they don't understand something. Ask, "Does this make sense to you?" What strategy can you use to help you understand?

Preparing for a Read-Aloud

Now let's get ready to walk through the steps of a read-aloud. Each session should be a fun and relaxing experience for the reader and listener alike, and ideally should be a daily, unrushed activity. It's important, therefore, to ensure you block off an appropriate amount of time, ideally fifteen to twenty minutes. (Although attention spans vary with every child!) This will give you enough time to talk about the book before, during, and after.

Here are some other ways to prepare for a read-aloud, to make the most of the experience.

Consider the Book You Choose

Selecting the perfect picture book sets the stage for a memorable read-aloud. Select books that are timely, relevant, and capable of sparking conversation, connection, or emotion. For instance, if students are being left out during recess, books about fairness and justice–*Each Kindness* by Jacqueline Woodson or *We're All Wonders* by R.J. Palacio. Others like *Strictly No Elephants* and *Say Something* can be used to discuss broader social concepts with older children. Perhaps students are struggling to practice patience, and reading aloud *Waiting* by Kevin Henkes or *The Very Impatient Caterpillar* by Ross Burach can help reteach the importance of the skill.

Look for stories that resonate with children's interests and developmental stages. This can include vibrant illustrations that captivate the eye and characters that resonate with the audience. Use books with rich language and diverse vocabulary to expand children's language skills and understanding. And don't shy away from reading books that are slightly above the children's current reading level. This can introduce them to new vocabulary and concepts and spark deeper interest and discussions. Additionally, children's listening comprehension is typically higher than their independent reading comprehension.

Pay attention to what is interesting children at the moment. Perhaps a recent visit to an aquarium or another book they read on a particular topic–such as the ever-popular dinosaurs!–can guide you to find a book that relates to those interests. This will help ensure they are excited about the book they are going to hear.

To help you find the ideal book for your read-aloud, Novel Effect creates Read-Aloud Calendars you can download from our website. These are carefully curated each year to provide tips for daily soundscapes from our library that coincide with particular monthly themes, such as Black History Month or Women's History Month, but also subjects like pets or space, and categories of book such as "guaranteed giggles." Our soundscapes are organized by similar categories on the app.

Practice Reading Beforehand

Preparation is key to a seamless read-aloud session. We suggest familiarizing yourself thoroughly with the chosen book by reading it multiple times, along with the accompanying soundscape. Pay attention to the flow of the text, pacing, and the nuances of character voices (more on how to "perform" a read-aloud later in this chapter). Practicing aloud helps you refine your delivery, ensuring fluency and confidence during the actual read-aloud. Taking time to practice will also help you anticipate questions or responses that may arise during the read-aloud, as well as where to stop and facilitate a brief conversation.

Create a Cozy Environment

A cozy, welcoming reading space will better relax children so they can focus and immerse themselves in the story. Minimize distractions by choosing a quiet corner or designated reading area, and arrange cushions or blankets. Ask the children to sit in a comfortable, read-aloud-ready position—for example, with criss-crossed legs. A calm atmosphere enhances children's ability to listen attentively and participate actively in discussions or activities connected to the story.

Introduce the Book to the Audience

Before you begin reading, take time to introduce the book to your listeners. Read the title and display the cover, pausing to discuss the illustrations. Ask the children to predict what the book might be about, and what makes them think so. Explain why you chose the particular book, and invite children to share how it might relate to their experiences.

Engaging the Audience As You Read

Engagement is crucial for a successful reading session, transforming a simple storytime into an immersive, fun experience. The following sections provide various strategies to make your reading sessions more interactive and engaging. From asking interesting questions and emphasizing key words to using sensory elements and soundscapes, these techniques will help you create a lively and memorable reading environment. Let's explore the ways you can encourage interaction and participation, ensuring that every reading session is both fun and enlightening for your audience.

Interactive Reading

Interaction should begin before you even open the book. Before reading, ask students about the book's cover, what they notice, and what they think the title means. Point out the name of the author and illustrator and ask whether they know any other books they have written or illustrated.

Pause to ask children what they think will happen next or how they feel about a character's actions. This keeps them engaged and thinking about the story. Do this throughout the reading, using the questions that gauge comprehension. For example, ask, "what do you think might happen next? What clues make you think so?"

If you are using a soundscape, you can ask, "Why do you think that particular music was playing, or that sound? How did that make you feel? What does that tell you about what is happening in the story, or how the characters are feeling?"

Encourage Interaction

Promote active participation by inviting children to interact with the story. Ask open-ended questions that encourage critical thinking and personal reflection. Prompt children to predict what might happen next or relate events to their own lives.

Have children make facial expressions, hand or body movements, or even call out when certain things happen. If the book incorporates counting like in *10 Spooky Pumpkins* or *100 Snowmen*, invite them to count along! If a book has repetitive words, like in *There Was an Old Lady* or If You Give series, invite them to call out the words, and fill in the lines as the story builds.

Pausing at strategic points allows time for children to share insights, discuss ideas with peers, and deepen their understanding of the story's themes. By fostering dialogue and exploration, you empower children to actively engage with literature, internalize story structures, and develop essential comprehension skills.

And remember: Soundscapes are prompted by your reading, at your own pace. They are not recordings you have to keep up with. So during reading, take your time to continue asking questions to maintain engagement and check comprehension.

Setting Up Successful Reading Partnerships for Young Children

To set young children up for success in reading partnerships, create a warm and structured environment where they can feel confident in exploring stories together. Begin by modeling what productive partner conversations look and sound like—showing them how to listen attentively, take turns, and build on each other's ideas. At first, provide clear guidance on who will start the conversation. You might choose a simple way to decide, such as by birth month, number of letters in their first name, or even by the color of their shirt. This removes uncertainty and helps children focus on sharing.

Set simple, engaging goals for each session, like talking about a favorite character or retelling the story in their own words. Introduce prompts to encourage conversation, such as "What was your favorite part?" or "Why do you think that happened?" Provide a time limit for each partner to speak so that conversations stay on track.

As children become more comfortable in their partnerships, add interactive activities like acting out scenes or drawing their favorite parts together to make the experience lively and memorable. Instead of celebrating milestones like finishing a book, encourage them to reflect on their conversation skills: ask them to show a thumbs up if they felt heard or to rate how well they and their partner stayed on topic by holding up a number on their fingers.

Involve the Senses

Engage multiple senses to enrich the reading experience. Use props such as puppets, stuffed animals, or visual aids to represent characters or key elements of the story. Create sound effects to enhance storytelling, mimicking actions or events described in the text. Encourage children to visualize scenes and characters, stimulating their imagination and making the narrative more vivid and memorable. By appealing to different senses, you create a multidimensional experience that enhances comprehension and enjoyment of the story.

Make it Interactive

Encourage children to participate actively by incorporating interactive elements into the read-aloud. Repeat refrains or chant rhymes together, inviting children to join in and contribute to the rhythm of the story. Create opportunities for call-and-response activities where children echo phrases or complete sentences from the book. Acting out parts of the story or role-playing scenes further immerses children in the narrative, making the reading session dynamic and engaging for everyone involved.

Use Soundscapes!

Feedback we receive at Novel Effect consistently highlights how our soundscapes are a game changer in capturing children's attention by creating concrete connections between the story and the listeners. Teachers love that Novel Effect's soundscapes help make lessons more engaging and interactive, and they appreciate the detailed activity packs that can be used across grade and reading levels and to support children in skills from sentence writing to science skills.

As described in Chapter 3, soundscapes work to layer understanding and comprehension, helping children recognize and feel the emotions intended in the story, whether it's humor, sadness, or tension. With careful attention particularly to illustrations, the soundscapes can highlight details that are not explicity stated in the text, adding another layer to the story and further aiding in both attention and comprehension in both the reader and the audience.

After Reading

You can begin by asking the children how the story or characters related to something that has happened in their life, or an experience they have had. If you've read books on a similar topic or by the same author in the past, you can ask how the stories are the same or different.

Extend the learning beyond the read-aloud session with engaging follow-up activities related to the book, available on the app or in packs at noveleffect.com (also see Part II of this book for a sampling).

Encourage children to express their creativity through arts and crafts projects inspired by characters or scenes from the story. Facilitate dramatic play activities where children reenact their favorite parts of the book or invent new endings. Foster writing skills by prompting children to write stories, journal entries, or letters to characters. Discussions about the themes, messages, or moral lessons of the book encourage critical thinking and deepen children's connection to literature. By integrating diverse activities, you reinforce comprehension, stimulate creativity, and nurture a lasting appreciation for storytelling among children.

Keep the book on display in the room where children can access it. After a read-aloud, children will often want to look through or read the book themselves. Depending on the teacher's preference, children can also read the book in combination with the soundscape; even for emerging readers or ELL students, our soundscapes are created to recognize a reader's voice with excellent accuracy, even if they are not ready with precise fluency.

Tips for "Performing" an Engaging and Fun Read-Aloud

Now that you've done your "before" reading preparation, it's time to get started with the actual read-aloud. Being an engaging reader is a skill that combines vocal variety and expressive facial and body language to bring a story to life. But you don't have to be a theatrical genius to get it right. By using your natural voice, adjusting volume, pacing, and pitch, and employing expressive facial gestures, you can make reading a captivating experience that highlights the drama, humor, sadness, or excitement of the book.

And remember to find ways to enjoy the read-aloud yourself. If you're having fun, the children are likely to have fun, too.

Use a Natural Voice

Keep your voice a natural as possible, and avoid "baby" talk. Overly cute voices can feel condescending to children. Your tone should instead reflect their intelligence, which will help keep them interested.

You can follow the lead of the author and the text to choose the voice to use. The words and mood of the story, if you pay attention carefully to them, will help guide your voice. If the text is playful, your voice can be light and lively. For serious moments, a more subdued tone is appropriate.

Vary Your Volume

Simply alternating from loud and soft to fit the narrative can add to the tension, sadness, humor, and drama of a story. Loud voices can signify excitement or danger, for example, while soft voices can create a sense of calm or intimacy. Whispering in particular can draw children in, making them feel like they're part of a secret or special moment in the story.

Alter Your Pacing

Vary the speed of your reading to match the action. Fast reading can convey excitement or urgency, while slowing down can help build suspense or emphasize important moments.

And pauses can be used very effectively. A well-timed pause can heighten anticipation, allow a moment to sink in, or give space for the child to react. Silence is a powerful tool to emphasize tension or sadness.

Change Your Pitch and Tone

Use a higher pitch for characters or moments of excitement and a lower pitch for serious or menacing scenes. Match your tone to the emotion of the scene. A warm, gentle tone can convey affection, while a stern tone can communicate seriousness or authority.

Incorporate Facial Expressions

Without overdoing it to the point where it's distracting to children or feels silly to you, there are some subtle ways, described below, that you can use your face to add to the tone, emotion, and action of the story to make your reading more active and engaging.

Emotive Expressions

Here are some simple ways to convey emotion in a story with your expressions.

- Eyes: Widen your eyes to show surprise or excitement. Narrow them to depict suspicion or concentration.
- Eyebrows: Raise your eyebrows for surprise or question, and furrow them for confusion or anger.
- Mouth: Smile for happy or humorous parts, and let your mouth drop open slightly for awe or shock. Pouting or frowning can indicate sadness or disappointment.

Body Language

You can more clearly convey action in a story with just a few subtle motions.

- Gestures: Use hand gestures to mimic actions in the story, like pointing to show direction or using your hands to depict size or shape.
- Posture: Lean forward to show engagement or excitement, and lean back for a moment of reflection or calm.

Mimicking Characters

Reading a story with multiple characters can be made far more entertaining (and make it more clear who is speaking) with a few changes in voice or factial expressions. Bringing characters to life in this way will hold a child's attention!

- Voice Matching: Slightly alter your voice to match different characters without overdoing it. A deeper voice for an adult character or a higher pitch for a child character can help distinguish who is speaking.
- Facial Adjustments: Change your facial expressions to match different characters' emotions. A happy character might have a big grin, while a sad character might have downturned lips and sad eyes.

Interview with Renee Belvis: Teaching ELL Students with Novel Effect

Although Novel Effect was designed primarily with elementary children in mind, Florida-based English-language-learner (ELL) educator Renee Belvis has found a new application: teaching baseball players English. She spoke with us about her work and how Novel Effect has been a successful tool in supporting it.

Novel Effect: We're thrilled to hear about how you're using Novel Effect with ELL students. What inspired you to start teaching English Language Learners? My journey into teaching ELL students began with a personal connection. My mother and older sisters immigrated to America from Germany in 1954 without knowing English. They faced significant challenges in school due to the lack of support for English language development while trying to maintain their native language, German. Witnessing their struggles and subsequent loss of their first language motivated me to ensure my students could retain their native language while acquiring English fluency. This dual-language approach became the cornerstone of my teaching philosophy, promoting bilingualism and cultural preservation.

Could you describe the setting where you teach and the unique challenges you encounter with your students?

I work with the international players of the Clearwater Threshers, a minor league baseball team affiliated with the Philadelphia Phillies, based in Florida. These young men, in their late teens and early twenties, come from diverse cultural and linguistic backgrounds. Many are far from home and navigating life in a new country, which presents challenges beyond language acquisition. The transient nature of their schedules, with frequent travel for games, limits consistent classroom time. Moreover, their primary access to technology is through personal smartphones, posing constraints for traditional educational tools.

How did you discover Novel Effect, and how has it become a valuable tool in your teaching toolkit?

I came across Novel Effect while searching for engaging content to enhance English learning for my ELL students. What initially drew me in was its ability to captivate and motivate these young athletes through immersive sound effects and music synchronized with read-alouds. Despite their age and varied educational backgrounds, the players responded enthusiastically to the auditory reinforcement provided by Novel Effect during reading sessions. This not only made the learning experience more enjoyable but also effectively supported their language development by reinforcing vocabulary and comprehension in a dynamic way.

Can you share a specific example of how Novel Effect has made a significant impact on your students' learning?

One standout moment involved a player named Felix Reyes, who struggled with English pronunciation. Using Novel Effect, Felix took the initiative to identify challenging words from his readings and practiced them repeatedly with the app's audio cues. The interactive nature of Novel Effect's soundscapes helped Felix build confidence in his spoken English by providing immediate auditory feedback. This not only improved his pronunciation but also boosted his overall reading fluency and comprehension.

How do you integrate Novel Effect into your lessons with the Clearwater Threshers?

I leverage Novel Effect in various ways to cater to different learning styles and schedules. For instance, I create read-aloud videos using Novel Effect for our pen pal exchanges with elementary school students in Wyoming, as part of a baseball-themed reading program. These videos not only showcase the players' progress in English but also foster connections with younger students who share a passion for baseball. Additionally, during in-person sessions, I preload iPads with Novel Effect's soundscapes for books available in twin-vision Braille. This allows players to practice reading independently while engaging with auditory cues that enhance their comprehension and enjoyment of the text.

What do you find most rewarding about using Novel Effect in your teaching practice?

As an educator, witnessing the players' genuine enjoyment and engagement with reading through Novel Effect is incredibly fulfilling. Despite their initial challenges with English, they eagerly participate in read-alouds and discussions, demonstrating improved confidence and language skills over time. Moreover, the app's versatility—accessible on smartphones, iPads, and computers—ensures that learning opportunities are maximized even amid the team's busy travel schedule.

Are there any particular challenges or barriers you've encountered in using Novel Effect, and how have you overcome them?

One of the primary challenges is ensuring equitable access to technology, as some players only have smartphones rather than laptops or iPads. While Novel Effect is compatible with smartphones, certain interactive features may be limited compared to larger screens. To address this, I optimize sessions by preloading materials and encouraging collaborative learning, where players can share devices during group activities. This fosters a supportive learning environment while maximizing the benefits of Novel Effect's auditory enhancements.

Looking ahead, how do you envision Novel Effect evolving in your teaching practice or expanding its impact?

Moving forward, I aim to further integrate Novel Effect into collaborative projects that promote literacy and cultural exchange among my ELL students.

Expanding our pen pal program and incorporating more diverse reading materials will allow us to explore different themes and genres while strengthening language skills and cross-cultural understanding. Additionally, I see potential in using Novel Effect to create personalized learning experiences tailored to individual player's interests and linguistic goals, enhancing their overall educational journey both on and off the field.

Finally, do you and your players have a favorite story or book that you've enjoyed using with Novel Effect?
The players particularly enjoy books like *Gibberish* by Young Vo, which resonates with them due to its relatable themes, and *I Promise* by LeBron James, a favorite among athletes for its inspirational message. These stories not only capture their interest but also encourage meaningful discussions about perseverance, teamwork, and personal growth.

Your innovative use of Novel Effect with the Clearwater Threshers illustrates the profound impact technology can have on language learning and community building.
I'm excited to continue exploring new ways to leverage Novel Effect's capabilities in empowering my students to excel both academically and personally.

Up Next . . .

We said at the start of this book that our goal with Novel Effect is to support all children in becoming readers, not just *at* grade level, but *above*, and we believe reading aloud with children, making the experience fun and social, is the best way to motivate them to become lifelong readers.

In this chapter, we shared what we've learned about making read-aloud sessions truly special—from preparation to the reading itself, and even activities afterward. Now it's time for you to experience the magic for yourself. We look forward to hearing about your experiences as you dive into the activities in Part II, explore the soundscapes on the app, and see how these tools can transform your read-aloud sessions into enjoyable, learning-rich adventures.

BRINGING STORIES TO LIFE

Welcome to Part II of this book, where we delve into the lessons and activities designed to bring the stories in the Soundscape Library to life. The books featured here are categorized by the following themes:

- Interact
- Laugh
- Love and Connection
- Move and Play
- Comfort and Acceptance
- Imagine and Create

You'll find detailed activities, discussion prompts, vocabulary, and extension exercises tailored to each book. We've also developed companion worksheets to enhance each lesson. Novel Effect app users can scan the QR code on the lesson page for instant access to the soundscape and companion worksheets. You can also download all worksheets at `www.noveleffect.com/rockyourreadaloud`.

The Book with No Pictures

by BJ Novak
Rocky Pond Books ©2014

The Story

This book turns the concept of read-alouds upside down with its playful and laugh-inducing approach! It's filled with silly words, sounds, and phrases that will have children in stitches, demonstrating the power of words and the fun of reading together. Perfect for encouraging even the most reluctant readers to engage and enjoy the magic of storytelling.

Read-Aloud Tips

Embrace the Silly: This book is filled with funny and nonsensical words, like "Boo Boo Butt" and playful phrases. Don't just lean into the silliness, embrace it! Use exaggerated expressions and a variety of tones to bring the words to life.

Interactive Engagement: The book often breaks the fourth wall, directly involving the reader. Encourage responses from your little learners, like laughing or repeating funny words, to make them feel part of the story.

Vocal Variety: Since the book pokes fun at the reader/narrator, using different voices for certain phrases or words can enhance the humor. For example, adopt a mock-serious tone when reading more absurd parts, or a robotic voice for any "robot monkey" references.

Pause for Effect: Give the children time to react to the humorous parts. Pausing after a particularly silly phrase or word can heighten the humor and make the experience more enjoyable.

Physical Expressions: Use gestures and facial expressions to complement the words. Since there are no pictures, your expressions and body language will help convey the story's playful nature.

Learning Concepts

imagination, humor, creativity, language, listening

Vocabulary

preposterous, utterly, ridiculous, glug, warning

Discussion Prompts

- This book has no pictures. How can you imagine the scenes just from the words?
- What was the silliest phrase in the book and why did it make you laugh?
- How did you feel when the book made the reader say silly things?
- If you could add a picture to this book, what would it be and why?
- How do you think the person reading the book felt about saying such silly things?
- Can you think of a silly sound that wasn't in the book? What is it? Where would you add it?
- Why do you think the author chose not to include pictures in this book?

- What do you think is the purpose of having a book with no pictures?
- How does this book compare to other books you've read? Is it more fun, less fun, or just different?
- Can words be just as fun as pictures? Why or why not?
- If you wrote a book with no pictures, what funny words would you include?
- Who do you want to read this book next? Why?

Extension Activity

Combining literacy skills and art to create their own "Book with No Pictures," students engage in a unique and interactive learning experience. They practice and enhance their writing, vocabulary, and storytelling skills by crafting their own narratives. Simultaneously, the project allows them to express their creativity and imagination.

At-Home Extension

Creating a homemade version of "The Book with No Pictures" is a fun and creative activity for a grown-up and child. Here are step-by-step directions for making your own book:

Materials Needed:
- Blank paper (several sheets)
- Markers, crayons, or colored pencils
- Stapler or ribbon/yarn (for binding)

Directions:

Prepare the Pages:
- Gather your blank paper. Decide on the size of your book. You can use the full sheet or fold them in half to create a smaller book.

Brainstorm Ideas:
- Sit down with the child and brainstorm ideas for your book. Think of silly words, phrases, and sentences that would be fun to read aloud. Remember, the sillier, the better!

Write the Story:

- Start writing your story on the blank pages. Let the child contribute with ideas and words. You can write on every page or just a few—it's up to you. Make sure to leave some space for illustrations, if desired.

Illustrate (Optional):

- Although *The Book with No Pictures* doesn't have illustrations, you can choose to add your own drawings. This could be abstract shapes, doodles, or anything that complements your silly story.

Decorate the Cover:

- Create a cover for your book. It should have the title and can be decorated however you like. The child can draw or write on the cover to personalize it.

Bind the Book:

- Once your pages are complete, put them in order and bind them. You can staple the pages along the edge to make a book. If you've folded the pages, you can staple along the fold. Alternatively, punch holes along the edge and tie the pages together with ribbon or yarn.

Read Together:

- Once your book is bound, it's time to read it together. Take turns reading the silly sentences and enjoy the laughter and fun.

Share Your Creation:

- If you're comfortable, share your homemade book with friends and family. It can be a great way to spread joy and laughter.

Press Here

by Herve Tullet
Chronicle Books ©2019

The Story

A delightful interactive experience that invites young readers to tap, shake, and tilt the book, watching in wonder as each action brings colorful dots to life on the pages. It's a fantastic tool for teaching cause and effect, encouraging imagination, and making reading a playful, hands-on adventure.

Read-Aloud Tips

Encourage Interaction: Each page invites the reader to take an action—pressing, shaking, tapping, blowing, or clapping. Encourage the children to perform these actions themselves. This physical interaction not only makes the book more enjoyable but also helps in developing their fine motor skills.

Use a Playful Voice: Since the book is about fun and interaction, use a playful and enthusiastic tone. Change your voice to match the actions—for example, a strong, excited voice for pressing and a gentle, whispering voice for blowing.

Build Anticipation: Before turning each page, build suspense about what might happen next. Ask questions like, "What do you think will happen if we press here?" This keeps the children engaged and makes them eager to see the results of their actions.

Teach Cause and Effect: Use this book as an opportunity to teach young children about cause and effect. Explain how their actions (like pressing or shaking the book) are causing the dots to change on the next page.

Make It a Group Activity: Project the book on your wall, letting the kids take turns reading the words and taking the actions. You'll see their eyes light right up with amazement, wondering if they now have superpowers.

Learning Concepts

cause and effect, fine motor, color recognition, creative thinking

Vocabulary

perfect, gently, fabulous, tilt, bravo

Discussion Prompts

- What was your favorite color used in the book and why?
- Recall a specific instruction from the book. What happened next?
- If you could add another action to the book, what would it be?
- How did pressing, shaking, or tilting the book make the story change?
- Which part of the book was the most surprising to you?
- How did the book make you feel? Happy, excited, curious?
- How is reading this book different from reading other books?
- What did you learn about colors and their mixing?
- Which action did you find the most fun: pressing, rubbing, or clapping?
- Would you like to read more books like this? Why or why not?

Extension Activity

This worksheet provides a canvas for young students to unleash their creativity. Each line offers a new opportunity to create a unique pattern, turning a simple activity into a vibrant exploration of art and imagination. This hands-on exercise not only complements the interactive nature of the book but also fosters fine motor skills and artistic confidence in young learners.

At-Home Extension

Create your own dot art story! This activity not only brings the book's concept to life but also encourages creativity, storytelling, and color exploration in a fun, hands-on way.

Materials Needed:
- A variety of colored paints or markers.
- Sheets of plain white paper.
- Cotton swabs or small paintbrushes for dot painting.

Directions:
- Set up a comfortable workspace with all the materials. Place sheets of white paper in front of both the child and the adult.

Read and Paint:
- As you read each page of *Press Here*, pause to create a similar scene on your paper. For example, when a page instructs you to press the yellow dot, both of you can paint a yellow dot on your paper.

Follow the Actions:
- When the book instructs to rub or press harder, discuss how you might show this in your artwork. Maybe press the swab down harder to make a bigger dot or smear the dot slightly.

Color Exploration:
- When the story introduces new colors, mix paints or use markers to create those colors on your paper.

Creative Expansion:

- Encourage the child to add their own twist to the story with additional dots or patterns. Maybe they want to add a green dot that wasn't in the book or create a pattern of dots around the original ones.

Storytelling with Art:

- As you progress, make up stories about the dots. Ask questions like, "What do you think the red dot is feeling?" or "Where is the blue dot going?"

Final Display:

- Once you finish reading the book and your dot artworks are complete, display them and talk about how each of you interpreted the instructions differently.

This Book Just Ate My Dog!

by Richard Byrne
Henry Holt and Co. ©2014

The Story

Embark on a whimsical adventure with a book that literally gobbles up its characters, creating a hilarious and unexpected interactive experience for young readers. This imaginative tale not only tickles the funny bone but also subtly teaches children about problem-solving and the joy of unpredictability in storytelling. Its playful approach to the physical book as part of the story is sure to engage children and adults alike, making it a fantastic choice for read-aloud sessions that are both entertaining and subtly educational.

Read-Aloud Tips

Encourage Participation: The book invites readers to interact with it, for example, by shaking the book to help release the characters. Encourage the children to participate in these actions. This physical engagement makes the reading experience more dynamic and fun.

Expressive Reading: Use varied and expressive tones to match the unfolding drama. Convey Bella's surprise, worry, and determination through your voice. This helps to build suspense and keeps the listeners engaged.

Visual Engagement: As the book cleverly uses its physical layout (such as characters disappearing into the gutter of the book), point out these visual elements to the children. This helps them understand the unique interaction between the text and the book's physical structure.

Discuss the Plot: Pause at key moments to discuss what's happening. Ask questions like, "What do you think will happen next?" or "How can we help Bella?" This not only aids comprehension but also makes the reading session more interactive.

Character Voices: Give different voices to the various characters that appear in the book, including Bella, Ben, and the rescue services. This adds an extra layer of fun and helps to distinguish each character.

Book Handling: Turn the book as directed by the text, like when the book needs to be shaken. This physical movement adds a playful element and demonstrates how books can be interactive objects.

Learning Concepts

problem-solving, humor, fine motor

Vocabulary

stroll, odd, investigate, vanish, ridiculous, appear, reappear, lovely, naughty

Discussion Prompts

- How did you feel when Bella's dog disappeared in the book? How do you think she felt?
- What would you do if you were Bella and your dog disappeared like that?

- When Ben went to help, he disappeared too! Were you surprised? Why or why not?
- How do you think shaking the book helped bring everyone back?
- If you could talk to the book, what would you say to it?
- This story was a bit different from other books. What made it special?
- How did you feel when everyone came back after shaking the book?
- After reading the book, where do you think the items went? Could this happen in real life? Why or why not?

Extension Activity

After reading *This Book Just Ate My Dog!* combine problem-solving and spatial awareness. Have students complete a puzzle to put Bella's dog back together correctly!

At-Home Extension

Collaboratively create a new story based on *This Book Just Ate My Dog*.

Materials Needed:
- The blank booklet provided.
- Crayons, colored pencils, or markers.
- A pencil or pen for writing.

Directions:

Read the Book Together:
- Start by reading *This Book Just Ate My Dog* together. Pay close attention to the characters, the plot, and how the story unfolds.

Brainstorm Ideas:
- Discuss with each other what could happen next in the story. Ask questions like, "What new adventure could Bella and her dog go on?" or "What if the book ate something else?"

Draw the Pictures:

- The child takes the lead in drawing the pictures and leading the new story.

Write the Story:

- Decide if the child or the grown-up will write the words. If the child is writing, the grown-up can help by spelling out words or giving ideas. If the grown-up is writing, let the child tell you what to write.

Share Your Story:

- Once you've finished, read your new story together. You can even share it with other family members or friends!

Tap the Magic Tree

by Christie Matheson
Greenwillow Books ©2013

The Story

An enchanting journey through the seasons, illustrated with a touch of magic in every page turn. This interactive book invites young readers to tap, rub, shake, and blow on the pages to assist in the tree's transformation through the seasons. It's an inventive way to teach children about nature's cycles, fostering a sense of wonder and participation. Perfect for engaging young minds in both reading and the natural world, this book is a delightful addition to any storytime, encouraging imagination and a love for the environment.

Read-Aloud Tips

Encourage Participation: The book invites readers to interact with it, for example, tapping, rubbing, or shaking the pages. Encourage the children to participate in these actions. This physical engagement makes the reading experience more dynamic and fun.

Emphasize the Transformation: Highlight the tree's transformation with enthusiastic commentary as the seasons change. Say things like, "Wow, look at how the tree is growing!" or "The leaves are falling, can you see them fluttering down?"

Predict Outcomes: Engage the children further by asking open-ended questions like, "What do you think will happen if we rub the tree?" or "What changes do you see in the tree now?"

Book Handling: Turn the book as directed by the text, like when the book needs to be shaken. This physical movement adds a playful element and demonstrates how books can be interactive objects.

Learning Concepts

seasons, cause and effect, fine motor, following directions

Vocabulary

bare, bud, forms, jiggle, petals, trunk, whoosh, patient

Discussion Prompts

- What does it mean to be "bare"? How can you tell the tree is bare?
- How did the tree change after we tapped it? Do you think trees can change like this in real life?
- What might happen after we rub the tree?
- Describe how the tree looks now compared to the beginning of the book.
- What do you think jiggling the tree will do?
- Why are we brushing away the petals? What season do you think it is now in the book?
- How has the tree changed throughout the story so far?
- What colors do you see on the tree?
- How does the snow change the tree? What season do you think it is now?
- What was your favorite part of the magic tree's journey? Why?

Extension Activity

Connect this interactive read-aloud to science standards! After reading, have students draw how a tree changes during each season. Afterwards, discuss the differences in each tree and why the students made those creative decisions.

At-Home Extension

After reading, help your child connect the concepts learned in the book with real-world observations, enhancing their understanding of nature and seasons.

Materials Needed:
- A copy of *Tap the Magic Tree* by Christie Matheson
- Notepad and pen/pencil for taking notes
- Camera or smartphone (optional, for taking pictures of trees)

Directions:

Read the Book Together:
- Take your time to discuss the illustrations and how the tree changes across different pages, representing different seasons.

Identify Your Current Season:
- After reading, have a conversation about the current season. Ask the child questions like, "What season is it now? How do you know?"

Find the Matching Season in the Book:
- Flip through *Tap the Magic Tree* and find the pages that represent the current season in your location.
- Discuss how the tree in the book looks during this season. Note characteristics like leaf color, presence of flowers or fruits, and overall appearance.

Outdoor Exploration:
- Go for a walk outside, aiming to find trees that match the description of the tree in the book for the current season.
- As you walk, encourage the child to observe the trees. Ask them to notice similarities and differences between the trees they see and the tree in the book. For example, "Does this tree have the same kind of leaves as the one in our book? What's different about it?"

Discussion and Comparison:
- While walking, or after returning home, have a discussion about what was observed.
- Encourage the child to talk about which real-life tree resembled the tree in the book the most and why.
- If the child took notes or pictures, use these to help recall and compare the trees.

Reflective Drawing or Journaling (Optional):
- Back at home, the child can draw their favorite tree they saw during the walk, trying to capture how it looks in the current season.
- Alternatively, they can write a short journal entry about the experience, what they learned about trees, and how the seasons affect them.

If You're Scary and You Know It

by Carole Gerber
Familius ©2019

The Story

Clap your claws, gnash your teeth, and join in the monstrous fun with this playful twist on a familiar children's song. *If You're Scary and You Know It* combines catchy rhythms with an array of friendly, not-so-spooky monsters, making it a fantastic read for Halloween or any time of year. It's an excellent way to encourage children to embrace their playful side while learning about rhythm and participation in songs. The book's lively illustrations and engaging text are sure to have both kids and adults singing, stomping, and roaring along!

Read-Aloud Tips

- **Interactive Actions:** When you reach the part of the song where children are asked to "clap their claws" or "gnash their teeth," demonstrate the actions yourself and encourage them to copy you. Be exaggerated and playful with your movements to show that it's all about fun.

- **Rhythmic Pauses:** Use pauses between verses for suspense. After singing "If you're scary and you know it..." stop, look around as if searching for the monsters, then shout the next action like "ROAR!" to surprise and delight the kids.
- **Create Monster Voices:** Use different voices for each type of monster. Try growling, squeaking, or roaring for added fun. Let the kids imitate those voices to increase their participation.
- **Invite Group Participation:** Ask the group, "Who can clap their claws the loudest?" or "Who has the scariest gnash?" to encourage playful competition. Make sure to praise everyone for their scary (and silly!) efforts.

Learning Concepts

emotion recognition, musical rhythm, social interaction

Vocabulary

moan, groan, greedy, jig, aboard, brew, potion, cauldron, fiendish, cloak, prey, twitch, frightful, crop, bony

Discussion Prompts

- What spooky actions do the characters do in the book?
- What new words have you heard so far?
- Why rhyming words have you heard so far?
- What funny things would you put in a witch's brew?
- What does it mean to be fiendish? Can you make a fiendish smile?
- If you were a scarecrow, how would you scare the birds away?
- How would you dress up if you were in this book?
- If you were in this book, what would your page sound like?
- What is your favorite part of the book and why?

Extension Activity

Let students become authors! Have each student design a page that shows their personality using the same text structure as Carole Gerber.

At-Home Extension

Reinforce reading comprehension and encourage imaginative play by acting out the scenes from the book.

Materials Needed:
- A copy of the book *If You're Scary and You Know It*
- Comfortable space to move around

Directions:

Cozy Reading Time:
- As you read, encourage the child to listen closely to the descriptions of the characters and their actions.

Prepare for Action:
- After the initial reading, take a few minutes to discuss the various characters in the book.

Re-read and Act:
- The grown-up will re-read the book. This time, as each character is introduced and their actions described, pause to give the child a moment to act it out.
- Encourage the child to use their imagination. For instance, they can moan and groan for a ghost, dance like a pirate, or pretend to mix a witch's brew.

Involvement:
- Ask the child to predict what action is coming next if they remember it from the first read.

Reflection and Discussion:
- After finishing the book, spend a few minutes discussing which character was their favorite to act out and why.
- Ask them if they would do anything differently if they were that character.

Repeat for More Fun:
- If the child shows interest, you can read and act out the book again, perhaps switching roles or adding different interpretations to the characters' actions.

Don't Let the Pigeon Drive the Bus

by Mo Willems

Hyperion Books for Children ©2003

The Story

This delightful tale, with its simple yet expressive illustrations, invites young readers into a humorous negotiation with a persistent pigeon dreaming of driving a bus. Its interactive style encourages children to voice their thoughts, fostering decision-making and moral reasoning. Perfect for read-aloud sessions, it not only tickles the funny bone but also subtly teaches the importance of rules and responsibility, making it a hit in classrooms and bedtime reading alike.

Read-Aloud Tips

- **Set the Tone with Excitement:** Begin by telling the children that they're about to help with an important task—making sure the pigeon doesn't drive the bus! Build up anticipation for their role in the story.

- **Use a Distinct Voice for the Pigeon:** Give the pigeon a unique, playful voice that shows his enthusiasm and desperation. This adds humor and helps distinguish the pigeon's character from the narrator.
- **Encourage Active Participation:** From the start, remind the children that they are in charge of saying "no" to the pigeon. Ask them, "Will you let the pigeon drive the bus?" and wait for their responses. Encourage loud and enthusiastic "No!" answers.
- **Exaggerate the Pigeon's Pleas:** As the pigeon becomes more desperate, exaggerate his voice, expressions, and body language. Make him whine, plead, and bargain in silly ways to get the kids laughing while reinforcing their role in stopping him.
- **Pause for Effect:** After each of the pigeon's pleas or tricks, pause to give the children time to react and shout their responses. Use their enthusiasm to drive the pacing of the book.

Learning Concepts

social emotional learning, persuasion, responsibility, humor

Vocabulary

pigeon, steer, careful, block

Discussion Prompts

- What is a pigeon? Where have you seen one before?
- Where do you think the bus driver is going?
- Why do you think the bus driver does not want the pigeon driving the bus?
- How can you tell the pigeon wants to drive the bus badly?
- Why do you think the pigeon wants to drive the bus so badly?
- What new idea do you think the pigeon has at the end? How can you tell?
- Where do you think the pigeon would drive to in the truck?
- What might he carry in a big truck?

Extension Activity

After reading *Don't Let the Pigeon Drive the Bus*, students work on an imaginative activity to extend the series with their own unique book. This learning experience is designed to cultivate brainstorming, creativity, and literacy skills.

At-Home Extension

Grab your paints or markers! Your little learner will use fine motor skills to create their own pigeon character.

Play This Book!

by Jessica Young
Bloomsbury Children's Books ©2018

The Story

This interactive story turns reading into a playful adventure, inviting children to tap, spin, and jiggle along with the book's pages. It's an inventive way to engage young readers, encouraging not only physical interaction but also imagination and a love for books as more than just stories. Ideal for energetic read-aloud sessions, this book is a wonderful tool for fostering fine motor skills and a sense of rhythm in young children, while also promoting a love of reading through play.

Read-Aloud Tips

- **Set the Stage for Play:** Let the children know this book isn't just for reading–it's for playing! Get them excited about the physical actions they'll be doing as you move through the pages.
- **Demonstrate the Movements:** As you read, demonstrate each action (tapping, spinning, jiggling) and encourage the children to copy you. Use exaggerated movements to make it fun and easy for them to follow along.

- **Invite Full Participation:** Encourage every child to take part, saying things like, "Okay, everyone, let's tap together!" or "Who can spin the fastest?" This promotes group involvement and keeps the energy up.
- **Match Actions to Rhythm:** As the book incorporates rhythm, keep a steady beat when asking the kids to tap or spin. You can even introduce simple clapping or snapping to enhance the rhythmic aspect of the story.
- **Use Different Voices and Sounds:** Add playful sound effects and change your tone for different parts of the book. For example, you could use a soft, quiet voice for delicate tapping or a loud, excited voice for spinning, matching the mood to the action.

Learning Concepts

music and rhythm, fine motor, creative play

Vocabulary

band, lend, strum, beat, keys, rhythm, drum, guitar, maracas, saxophone, rattle, trombone, bravo, pro, bow, cymbals

Discussion Prompts

- Show me how you would play the guitar. What body parts are you using?
- Let's pretend to play the drums! Tap to create a rhythm.
- What do piano keys look like?
- The trombone has a slide; show how you would move it!
- Did you feel like a part of the band while reading this book? Why or why not?
- Which instrument was your favorite? Why?
- What kind of music do you think this band would play?
- How do you think the different instruments work together to make music?

- If you could add another instrument to the band, what would it be and why?
- What do you think the band name should be? Why?

Extension Activity

After reading *Play This Book*, strengthen fine motor skills and story recall while reviewing musical elements with our extension activity.

At-Home Extension

Create and replicate rhythms, practicing your child's listening skills, concentration, and musicality.

Materials Needed:
- Any available objects that can be used as makeshift instruments (e.g. pots and pans for drums, spoons for tapping, empty bottles for blowing across the tops)
- Enthusiasm and a good ear for music!

Directions:

Set Up the Instruments:
- Gather your makeshift instruments and sit facing each other.

Choose the Leader:
- Decide who will start as the rhythm leader. This role will alternate between the grown-up and the child.

Create a Rhythm:
- The leader starts by creating a simple rhythm using their chosen "instrument." This rhythm should be short and easy enough to be remembered and replicated, especially keeping in mind the child's ability.

Echo the Rhythm:
- The other player listens carefully and then tries to replicate the exact rhythm. They can use the same "instrument" or a different one to add variety.

Switch Roles:
- After each turn, switch roles so both get a chance to create and copy rhythms.

Gradually Increase Complexity:
- As the game progresses, gradually make the rhythms more complex or faster, challenging each other's listening and replication skills.

Add Variations:
- Introduce variations where you combine rhythms or movements to make the game more fun and engaging.

Reflection:
- After the game, talk about which rhythms were easy or hard and why. Discuss the different sounds each "instrument" made.

Dragons Love Tacos

by Adam Rubin
Dial Books ©2012

The Story

In this whimsically illustrated and engaging tale, children discover the quirky love dragons have for tacos. The story serves as a fun gateway into exploring culinary tastes and the humorous consequences of spicy food, making it perfect for interactive read-alouds. It's not just a feast for the imagination but also a delightful way to introduce young readers to the joys of diverse foods and the importance of understanding others' preferences, all wrapped in a bundle of giggles and dragon-filled fun.

Read-Aloud Tips

Engage with Humor: The book is filled with whimsical and silly moments. Use a playful and lively tone to match the humor in the story. Don't be afraid to be a bit dramatic to bring out the fun.

Visual Descriptions: As you read, describe the illustrations in detail. Since dragons and tacos are visually engaging for children, pointing out the colorful and quirky details can enhance their listening experience.

Character Voices: Give the dragons distinct voices to make them more vivid in the listeners' imaginations. You could use deep, growly voices or high, excited ones depending on the dragons' personalities as you interpret them.

Interactive Questions: Ask questions like, "What kind of tacos do you think dragons like best?" or "How would you throw a taco party for dragons?" This involvement will keep the children engaged and let them use their imaginations.

Emphasize the Key Moments: Highlight the crucial parts of the story, especially the hilarious consequences of feeding spicy salsa to dragons. Build up to these moments with suspense and excitement in your voice.

Follow the Dragons' Emotions: Reflect the dragons' emotions in your reading. When they're happy about tacos, sound joyful; when they encounter spicy salsa, show their surprise and discomfort.

Learning Concepts

predictions, cause and effect, self-regulation

Vocabulary

gigantic, sizzling, crispy, tortilla, mild, accordion, speck, samaritan

Discussion Prompts

- Why do you think dragons love tacos so much?
- How does the host of the taco party make a mistake?
- Why is reading the "fine print" important?
- How did the dragons react to the spicy salsa?

- How do you think the host felt when the dragons ate the spicy tacos?
- What does the story tell us about making mistakes and fixing them?
- What silly sound effects did you hear in the Novel Effect soundscape?
- Would you want to have a taco party with dragons? Why or why not?
- What lesson did the host of the party learn by the end of the story?
- Why do you think the dragons helped rebuild the house?
- How might the story have been different if the host had read the fine print?
- Why is it important to know the preferences of our guests when hosting a party?

Extension Activity

Spice up this read-aloud with a craftivity your students will devour! Combine fine motor skills and writing for a perfect combination!

At-Home Extension

Cook up family fun after reading *Dragons Love Tacos*.

Directions:

Discuss the Story:
- Begin by discussing the story.

What was your favorite part of the story?
- How would you feel if you were at the dragon's taco party?
- What toppings would you put on a dragon-friendly taco?

Go Grocery Shopping:
- Together, decide on the ingredients you want in your tacos. Let the child decide on a special ingredient they might want to try, just like in the story.

Cook Together:

- Prepare the taco ingredients together. Depending on the child's age, they can help with washing vegetables, grating cheese, or setting the table. Safety first: ensure any tasks given to the child are age-appropriate.
- Once all ingredients are ready, come together and assemble your tacos.

Enjoy:

- Sit down and enjoy your tacos! Talk about the flavors and the fun you had making them. Discuss the similarities or differences between your taco night and the one in the book.

We Don't Eat Our Classmates

by Ryan T. Higgins
Disney Hyperion ©2018

The Story

This amusing and relatable story, filled with vibrant illustrations, tackles the universal theme of fitting in, but with a humorous twist featuring a dinosaur protagonist. It's a playful way to discuss empathy, friendship, and the golden rule with young readers. Ideal for classroom read-alouds, this book not only incites laughter but also opens up conversations about treating others kindly and understanding feelings, making it a valuable tool for social and emotional learning in a fun, memorable way.

Read-Aloud Tips

Expressive Characterization: Penelope requires a distinct voice to match her playful and mischievous character. You can also use different voices for other characters like the teacher, Mrs. Noodleman, to bring the story to life.

Emphasize Humor: Spoiler alert—Penelope eats her classmates! Use a lighthearted and humorous tone to highlight when the feasting begins, and don't be afraid to be a little theatrical.

Visual Descriptions: The book's illustrations add a lot to the story. Describe the pictures vividly, especially the expressions of Penelope and her classmates, to help the children imagine the scenes.

Discuss the Moral: After reading, talk about the book's message. Discuss why it's not okay to eat classmates (it isn't, right?) and the importance of empathy, as Penelope learns when she experiences being eaten by the class goldfish.

Learning Concepts

empathy, understanding differences, social-emotional learning, problem-solving, language skills, comprehension, and creative expression.

Vocabulary

extinct, delicious, determined, lonely, appetite, peek

Discussion Prompts

- Why do you think Penelope ate her classmates?
- What should she have done instead?
- Why does Penelope struggle to make friends with her classmates?
- How do you think Penelope's classmates feel when she stops eating them?
- Would you be nervous if Penelope was your classmate? Why or why not?
- How did Penelope's feelings change throughout the story?
- Why is it important to treat our classmates with kindness and respect?

- Can you relate to any of the challenges Penelope faces? How so?
- What does Penelope learn about the value of friendship?
- How does the story teach us about empathy and seeing things from different perspectives?
- What important lessons can we learn from Penelope?
- Which parts of the Novel Effect soundscape made you laugh?
- How did the soundscape help you understand how she was feeling?

Extension Activity

After reading *We Don't Eat Our Classmates*, have students complete a Penelope Rex craft that incorporates fine motor skills, reading comprehension, and writing. Then showcase your students' work on your bulletin board!

At-Home Extension

During this activity, children will foster creativity, empathy, and understanding of friendship in a fun and interactive way with their grown up.

Directions:

Setting the Stage:
- After reading *We Don't Eat Our Classmates* discuss the main character, Penelope Rex, and her unique challenges in making friends.

Role Assignment:
- The adult plays the role of Penelope Rex, while the child takes on the role of one of her classmates. If there are more family members or friends, they can join as additional classmates.

Scenario Creation:
- Together, come up with a fun and imaginative scenario where Penelope Rex tries to make friends. Encourage the child to think creatively about how Penelope can

show kindness and friendship without resorting to her dinosaur instincts.

Role-Playing:

- Act out the scenario you've created. Use props or costumes if you have them to make the role-playing more engaging. The focus should be on positive interactions and the demonstration of friendly behavior.

Discussion:

- After the role-playing, have a discussion about the experience. This is a great opportunity for the adult to impart lessons about empathy, kindness, and the importance of treating others well.

Ask questions like:

- "How do you think Penelope felt trying to make friends?"
- "What are some good ways to show someone you want to be their friend?"

The Wonky Donkey

By Craig Smith
Scholastic Inc. ©2010

The Story

This hilariously quirky story, with its catchy rhythm and playful language, introduces children to a very special donkey with a host of delightful oddities. It's a fantastic pick for read-aloud sessions, encouraging laughter, participation, and the joy of silly wordplay. Beyond its humor, the book subtly teaches lessons about acceptance and celebrating uniqueness, making it not only a source of giggles but also a heartwarming tale that promotes the value of embracing differences in ourselves and others.

Read-Aloud Tips

Emphasize the Rhymes and Rhythm: The book has a fantastic rhythmic quality due to its rhyming words. Make the most of this by reading with a musical, sing-song voice. You might even tap your foot or gently clap to the rhythm as you read, encouraging the children to join in. Of course, Novel Effect really shines in this story to keep you on beat!

Play with Vocal Variety: Each new description of the donkey adds a fun adjective to his character (like "wonky," "winky," "honky-tonky," etc.). Change your voice tone with each addition. Start with a normal tone for "wonky" and then add excitement, surprise, or silliness as you stack up the adjectives.

Encourage Participation: Pause before the end of each rhyming phrase to let the children fill in the blank. For example, when you get to "He was a wonky donkey. . ." stop and see if the kids shout out "wonky!" It's a great way to keep them engaged and listening closely.

Mimic the Donkey's Actions: If the donkey is winking, give a big wink. If he's honky-tonking, pretend to play a piano or dance a little jig. These actions will not only make the story come alive but also provide visual entertainment for your audience.

Build Anticipation: As the story progresses and the donkey becomes more and more "wonky," build up the anticipation. Slow down your reading speed a bit, add suspense to your voice, and then reveal the next adjective with a flourish.

Laugh and Enjoy: Your enjoyment is contagious. Don't be afraid to laugh at the silly parts. Children love seeing adults enjoy the humor in their books.

Learning Concepts

joy of reading, language development through repetition and rhyme, the musicality of language, memory and cognitive skills

Vocabulary

wonky, slim, lanky, mischief, spunky

Discussion Prompts

- How do you think the donkey felt about having three legs?
- What made this donkey different from other donkeys?

- Make up three words that rhyme with "wonky."
- Why do you think the donkey likes country music?
- How would you describe the donkey's personality?
- Which part of the donkey's description did you find the funniest?
- How did the donkey's appearance change throughout the book?
- If you could add another feature to the donkey, what would it be?
- Can you think of two new rhyming words to describe the donkey?
- How do you think the donkey's story might continue after the book?

Extension Activity

After reading *The Wonky Donkey*, reinforce rhyming and listening skills with a fun whole group activity.

Circle Formation:
- Arrange students in a circle.

Game Introduction:
- Explain that they will be creating new rhyming names for the donkey from the book *The Wonky Donkey*.

Starting the Game:
- The teacher begins by saying, "He was a . . ."
- The first student then adds two rhyming words, like "happy sappy."
- The next student adds another set of rhyming words, for example, "funny runny," and so on.

Continuation:
- The game continues with each student adding their unique set of rhyming words.

Ending the Game:
- The teacher concludes by saying, "donkey."

Adaptions for Older Students:
- Before adding their two rhyming words, each student must first recite all the previous names in order. For example, if the last student said "happy sappy," the next student starts by saying "He was a happy sappy, funny runny . . ."

At-Home Extension

After reading *The Wonky Donkey*, foster creativity and reinforce rhyming skills with your little learner.

Choose an Animal:
- The child starts by choosing their favorite animal, for example, a cat, dog, or elephant.

Creating a Rhyming Name:
- The adult begins by saying, "Here is a [animal], and it's not just any [animal], it's a . . ."
- The child then adds two words that rhyme to describe the animal, such as "fluffy puffy" for a cat or "biggy wiggly" for an elephant.
- The adult then repeats the phrase with the child's additions, for example, "Here is a cat, and it's not just any cat, it's a fluffy puffy cat."

Adding More Descriptions:
- The game continues with the adult and child taking turns to add more rhyming words to describe the animal.
- Each time, the phrase is repeated from the beginning with all the added descriptions.

Creating a Story:
- Each new set of rhyming words can be used to build a small story around the animal. For example, if the child says "sleepy weepy" for a bear, they could add a sentence like, "because it was time for its winter nap."

Ending the Game:
- The game can end whenever the child wishes, or when it becomes too challenging to add more rhymes.

The Serious Goose

····

by Jimmy Kimmel
Random House Books for Young Readers ©2019

The Story

This engaging and humorous story invites young readers into an interactive experience, trying to make a very serious goose smile. With its vibrant and expressive illustrations, the book offers a delightful exploration of emotions and the power of playfulness. Ideal for read-alouds and interactive sessions, it not only incites giggles and participation but also provides a gentle way to discuss feelings and the importance of laughter. It's a charming tale that encourages children to be silly and imaginative, making reading a joyous and interactive adventure.

Read-Aloud Tips

Interactive Opening: The book begins by inviting readers to try to make the Serious Goose smile. Start by showing the cover and asking the children, "Do you think we can make this goose smile?" Get them excited about the challenge ahead.

Vary Your Tone for Different Characters: Use a deep, serious voice for the Serious Goose and a more animated, playful tone for the narrating parts. This contrast will help bring out the humor in the goose's steadfast seriousness.

Encourage Child Participation: This book is all about trying to make the goose laugh. Involve the children by asking them to make funny faces, noises, or gestures at the appropriate moments. You could say, "On the count of three, let's all make the silliest face we can to see if the goose laughs!"

Utilize the Mirror Effect: The book includes a mirror to try and make the goose laugh. Use this as an interactive element. Have the children look into the mirror and make funny faces. If reading to a group without access to the mirror in the book, you can bring a small hand mirror or encourage children to look at each other while making funny faces.

Dramatic Reading: Emphasize the phrases that are trying to make the goose laugh, like "I will make a silly face" or "I will wear a goofy hat." Make these moments stand out by changing your voice, acting out the actions, or even using props if you have them handy.

Expressive Facial Expressions and Gestures: Since the book is all about trying to change the goose's expression, be overly expressive yourself. Exaggerate your smiles, frowns, and looks of surprise to mirror the attempts to change the goose's mood.

Pause for Effect: Before revealing the goose's reactions on each page, pause and ask the children, "Do you think it worked?" Build a little suspense and get them guessing.

End on an Interactive Note: As the book concludes with the goose returning to being serious, ask the children, "Do you think we can keep our serious faces like the goose?" Challenge them to stay serious for a few seconds, then break into smiles and laughter, celebrating the fun you've had.

Learning Concepts

humor, emotional recognition, interactive and participatory reading, creativity, and cognitive skills

Vocabulary

serious, delicious, goofy, command, amuse, attorney

Discussion Prompts

- What was your favorite part of the story and why?
- How did the goose feel at the beginning of the book?
- Why do you think the goose didn't want to smile?
- Name some of the silly things that were done to make the goose smile.
- How did the goose change throughout the story?
- What finally made the goose smile?
- How do you think the goose felt after it smiled?
- If you were in the book, what would you do to make the goose smile?
- When is it important to be serious?
- When is it okay to be silly?
- Would you like to meet a goose like the one in the story? Why or why not?

Extension Activity

After reading *The Serious Goose*, extend the fun with a seriously silly activity to keep your students engaged.

At-Home Extension

Enjoy a silly game with your little learner! Attempt to make each other laugh using different means, inspired by *The Serious Goose*.

Taking Turns:
- The first person (Player A) tries to make the other (Player B) laugh by telling a joke, making a silly face, or performing a funny action.
- Player B must try to keep a serious face and not laugh.

Scoring:
- If Player B laughs, Player A gets a point.
- Then it's Player B's turn to try to make Player A laugh.

No Physical Contact:

- Remember, making the other person laugh must be done without any physical contact.

Game Duration:

- Decide on the length of the game beforehand, like a set number of rounds or a time limit.

Winning:

- The player with the most points at the end of the game is the winner.
- You can also play without keeping score, focusing instead on having fun and sharing laughs.

Love

by Matt de la Peña

G.P. Putnam's Sons Books for Young Readers ©2018

The Story

This profound and beautifully illustrated book takes young readers on a journey through various scenes depicting love in its many forms. From the love found in quiet moments at home to the shared joy in community gatherings, it paints a diverse and inclusive picture of love's presence in everyday life. This story not only captivates with its lyrical text and heartwarming illustrations but also opens up conversations about the importance of love, empathy, and connection in our lives, making it a valuable and touching read-aloud.

Read-Aloud Tips

Set the Tone with Your Voice: The book's lyrical and poetic style calls for a soothing and gentle reading voice. Start with a calm, soft tone to match the tenderness of the text. This helps create a cozy, intimate atmosphere for the story.

Encourage Emotional Connections: This book explores love in different scenarios, some joyful and some challenging. As you read, encourage the children to think about and share moments when they have felt loved or have shown love to others. This could be as simple as a hug, a kind word, or a shared experience.

Explore the Different Forms of Love: The story depicts love in various settings, from parental love to love in the community. Discuss these different forms of love with the children, asking them to identify moments in their lives that relate to the scenes in the book.

Use Expressive Reading to Highlight the Prose: The prose in *Love* is described as a meditation on love, transcending the usual narrative structure. Use expressive reading to highlight the poetic nature of the text. Vary your pace, tone, and volume to reflect the changing scenes and emotions.

Handle Sensitive Topics with Care: *Love* doesn't shy away from life's tougher moments. Be prepared to address these in a way that's appropriate for your audience's age and sensitivity.

End with a Positive Note: The book concludes on a hopeful, uplifting note. Emphasize this in your closing comments, reinforcing the idea that love is always present, even in difficult times.

Learning Concepts

emotional intelligence, literary appreciation, social themes, artistic expression

Vocabulary

figure, toddle, whisk, huddle, blare, dawn, gnarl, beacon, congregate

Discussion Prompts

- What does love feel like to you?
- How does love change in different parts of the book?
- What did you notice about the children and families in the book?

- Find a scene in the book that reminds you of a moment in your life.
- Why do you think the author chose to show love in so many different ways?
- How do the pictures help show the story's message?
- What does the love in your family look like?
- How can we show love to our friends at school?
- Do you think love can change over time? How?
- What scene in the book was your favorite depiction of love? Why?
- What are some small ways we can show love every day?
- If you could add a scene to the book, what would it be about?
- What did this book teach you about love?

Extension Activity

After reading, invite students to make text-to-self connections. They will illustrate, or write, their ideas inside the heart template to express the connections they made to their own life.

At-Home Extension

Materials Needed:
- Blank paper
- Coloring materials
- Writing utensils (pens or pencils)

Instructions:

Choose a Love Theme:
- Start by discussing with your child what aspect of love you want to depict. It could be a family moment, love for a pet, a kind gesture from a friend, or even a favorite place or activity that brings joy.

Sketch the Scene:
- Draw a scene on the paper that represents your chosen theme. Encourage creativity! It doesn't have to be perfect; it's about expressing your idea of love. Adults can help younger children with drawing if needed.

Add Color and Details:

- Use colors and any additional materials (like stickers or glitter) to bring your drawing to life. Discuss the choice of colors with your child—how do they relate to the feeling of love in your scene?

Write a Caption or Short Story:

- Beneath or beside your drawing, write a few sentences that explain the scene. This could be a description of what's happening, why it's a representation of love, or even a short, narrative story. Younger children can dictate their thoughts for parents to write if they're not yet comfortable with writing.

Discuss Your Artwork:

- Once the drawing and writing are complete, take some time to talk about what's been created. Why did you choose this scene? How does it make you feel? This part of the activity is great for bonding and understanding each other's perspectives on love.

Display Your Work:

- Find a special place in your home to display the artwork. It could be on the refrigerator, a bulletin board, or framed in a common area. This serves as a lovely reminder of the time spent together and the diverse meanings of love.

Hair Love

....

by Matthew A. Cherry
Kokila ©2019

The Story

This heartwarming story, with its beautiful illustrations, celebrates the special bond between a father and daughter through the lens of hair care. It's a tender portrayal of familial love, self-acceptance, and the beauty of African American hair. This book not only entertains with its charming narrative but also fosters conversations about cultural identity, diversity, and the importance of self-esteem. It's a delightful and meaningful read that resonates with both children and adults, highlighting the joys and challenges of personal expression.

Read-Aloud Tips

Convey the Warmth of the Relationship: The core of this story is the loving relationship between a father and his daughter. As you read, emphasize the warmth and care in their interactions. Use a tender and affectionate voice when reading the father's words and a cheerful, lively tone for the daughter, Zuri.

Highlight the Hair-Styling Process: The book focuses on the father doing his daughter's hair. Mimic the actions described in the book, like combing, braiding, or twirling your fingers as if playing with hair. This physical mimicry can help bring the story to life.

Discuss the Illustrations: Vashti Harrison's illustrations are vibrant and full of detail. Take time to explore these with the children. Point out the expressions on the characters' faces, the different hairstyles, and the cozy home setting. Ask questions like, "How do you think Zuri feels about her hair?" or "What do you notice about the father's expressions?"

Explore the Theme of Perseverance: The father in the story encounters challenges while doing Zuri's hair but keeps trying. Emphasize this aspect of the story, highlighting the message of perseverance and the importance of trying, even when things are difficult.

Encourage Participation with Repetitive Phrases: There are phrases in the book that are repeated, such as descriptions of Zuri's hair. Encourage children to repeat these phrases with you. This not only makes the reading interactive but also reinforces the positive messages about natural hair.

Use Expressive Facial Expressions and Body Language: Show struggle or frustration when the father is having a hard time with the hair, and joy and pride when they succeed.

Learning Concepts

self-esteem, family relationships, creative expression, respect and acceptance, cultural appreciation

Vocabulary

kink, coil, funky, professional, beam

Discussion Prompts

- What is the main idea of the story *Hair Love*?
- How does Zuri feel about her hair at the beginning of the story?
- What challenges does Zuri's father face when doing her hair?

- How does Zuri's father show his love and care for her through her hair?
- How does Zuri's mood change throughout the story, and why?
- What does this story teach us about family and support?
- How does the story show that it's okay to try new things, even if they are challenging?
- Why was it a special day for Zuri and her family?
- How does Zuri feel when her hair is finally done the way she likes it?
- What do you think is the significance of the title *Hair Love*?
- Can you relate to Zuri's experience in any way? How?
- What did you learn about hair and self-expression from this story?

Extension Activity

Encourage student creativity and innovation! This project, inspired by *Hair Love*, allows students to invent and illustrate a unique hair tool or accessory, fostering both their artistic and writing skills. It's a wonderful way to engage them in creative thinking and celebrate individuality and self-expression.

At-Home Extension

Celebrate and explore the creativity and bonding in hair styling, inspired by the themes of family and self-expression in *Hair Love*.

Materials Needed:
- Hair styling tools (combs, brushes, hair ties, clips, headbands, etc.)
- Safe and washable hair accessories (ribbons, temporary hair colors, non-toxic glitter)
- Mirror
- Camera or smartphone to take before and after photos
- Optional: Hair care products suitable for the child's hair type

Instructions:

Initial Discussion:
- Begin by discussing the story of *Hair Love* and how Zuri's unique hair is an integral part of her identity. Emphasize the special bond formed through the act of hair styling.

- Talk with the child about their own hair—what they like about it, any favorite styles they have or want to try.

Setting Up Your "Salon":

- Arrange a comfortable space with all your hair styling tools and accessories. You can even create a salon-like atmosphere by naming your salon and setting up a small styling station.

Choosing Hairstyles:

- Together, decide on a hairstyle to try. You can get inspiration from the book, look up simple and fun hairstyles online, or come up with your own creative ideas.

Hair Styling Session:

- Take turns being the stylist and the client. As you style each other's hair, talk about what you are doing and why you think it's a good style for the person.
- Be gentle and mindful of each other's comfort. It's a great opportunity to teach the child about gentle hair handling and care.

Photo Session:

- Once you both are happy with your hairstyles, have a photo session. Take before and after photos to capture the transformation.
- You can even make funny or stylish poses to add to the fun.

Reflecting on the Experience:

- After the salon day, talk about what you both enjoyed in the process. Discuss how hairstyles can be a form of self-expression and creativity.
- This is also a perfect time to reinforce positive messages about individuality and self-confidence related to one's appearance.

Stellaluna

by Janell Cannon
Clarion Books ©1993

The Story

This enchanting and beautifully illustrated tale follows a young bat's journey after being separated from her mother, leading to an unexpected friendship with birds. It's a captivating exploration of identity, acceptance, and the beauty of embracing differences. Ideal for classroom and bedtime reading, this story not only delights with its heartwarming narrative but also offers educational insights into bat behavior and encourages discussions about respect for diversity and the value of being true to oneself. It's a timeless read that combines adventure, empathy, and the wonders of the natural world.

Read-Aloud Tips

Create Distinct Voices for Characters: Give Stellaluna, the birds, and other characters their own unique voices. For Stellaluna, use a curious and sometimes confused tone, reflecting her journey of self-discovery. For the birds, consider using chirpier, more excitable tones.

Highlight the Contrasts Between Bats and Birds: As you read, emphasize the differences in how bats and birds live, like sleeping upside down or eating fruit versus insects.

Use Expressive Facial Expressions and Gestures: Reflect Stellaluna's emotions and the birds' reactions through your facial expressions and body language. Show surprise, confusion, and happiness at different points in the story to engage your young audience.

Discuss the Theme of Acceptance and Friendship: As you read, highlight the themes of acceptance and friendship. Talk about how despite their differences, Stellaluna and the birds care for and accept each other. This can lead to a discussion about the importance of accepting others who may be different from us.

Emphasize the Reunion Scene: The reunion between Stellaluna and her mother is a pivotal moment. Read this part with warmth and excitement, highlighting the joy of finding one's family and understanding one's identity.

Learning Concepts

Identity, friendship and acceptance, family, resilience, understanding differences and similarities

Vocabulary

sultry, croon, scent, ripe, shriek, limp, clutch, tremble, downy, startle, clamber, graceful, clumsy, anxious, peculiar, perch,

Discussion Prompts

- How did Stellaluna feel when she was separated from her mother?
- How did the baby birds react when Stellaluna first arrived in their nest?
- Can you think of a time when you felt different from others, like Stellaluna did? How did you handle it?

- What are some of the differences between Stellaluna and the baby birds?
- Why did Stellaluna try to act like a bird?
- How did Stellaluna change after she met the birds?
- What did Stellaluna learn about herself by the end of the story?
- What would you do if you were in Stellaluna's situation?
- How do you think Stellaluna felt when she reunited with her mother?
- How do you think the story would be different if Stellaluna had landed in a different animal's nest?
- What is the main message or lesson of the story?

Extension Activity

Using this craftivity inspired by *Stellaluna*, students create a rocking bat paper craft. They start by coloring in a bat, adding their personal touch to Stellaluna. Once they finish, they glue the bat's head onto the craft, assembling a 3D creation that rocks back and forth. This hands-on activity allows students to explore the story in an interactive way while developing fine motor skills and fostering creativity.

At-Home Extension

Review science and literacy skills through a compare and contrast activity with your little learner!

Materials Needed:
- A piece of paper
- Coloring supplies
- A copy of the *Stellaluna* book (for reference)

Instructions:

Preparation:
- Sit down with your child and briefly discuss what they remember about bats and birds from the story of Stellaluna. This can include their physical characteristics, habits, and habitats.

Drawing the Venn Diagram:
- Draw two large overlapping circles on the paper, creating a Venn diagram.
- Label one circle "Bats" and the other "Birds."

Filling in the Diagram:
- In the "Bats" circle, write down characteristics unique to bats (e.g. nocturnal, hang upside down).
- In the "Birds" circle, note down traits specific to birds (e.g. build nests, lay eggs).
- In the overlapping section, list similarities between bats and birds (e.g. both have wings, can fly).

Discussion and Learning:
- As you fill in the diagram, discuss each point with your child. Encourage them to think critically about why certain characteristics are unique or shared.
- You can reference the *Stellaluna* book to reinforce these concepts and make connections back to the story.

Creative Extension:
- Encourage your child to draw or color pictures of bats and birds around the Venn diagram. This adds a creative element to the activity and makes the learning experience more engaging.

Conclusion:
- Once the Venn diagram is complete, spend some time reviewing it together. Ask your child what new things they learned about bats and birds and how they can relate this knowledge back to the story of Stellaluna.

Love Monster

by Rachel Bright
Farrar, Straus and Giroux ©2014

The Story

A charming and colorful tale about a slightly hairy monster in a world of cute, fluffy creatures, searching for someone who will love him just the way he is. This delightful story offers a heartwarming perspective on love, acceptance, and the importance of being true to oneself. It not only entertains with its engaging narrative and vibrant illustrations but also teaches children about the value of self-acceptance and the power of persistence in finding where they belong. It's a sweet and uplifting read that resonates with anyone who's ever felt a little different.

Read-Aloud Tips

Emphasize the Character's Emotions: The Love Monster goes through a range of emotions in his quest to find love. Use different tones and expressions to convey his feelings of loneliness, hope, disappointment, and joy.

Encourage Empathy: Engage the children by asking questions like, "Have you ever felt like the Love Monster?"

Use Expressive Gestures: Mimic the actions of the Love Monster with your hands and body. For instance, when he's looking high and low for love, stretch your arms up high and then bend down low.

Vary Your Voice: Use a soft, gentle voice when the Love Monster is feeling sad or lonely, and a bright, excited tone when there's a turn of events or when he's feeling hopeful. This vocal variety adds to the emotional impact of the story.

End on a Positive Note: The story has a happy and reassuring ending. Conclude your reading by reiterating the message that love can be found in the most unexpected places and times, and that everyone is deserving of love.

Learning Concepts

acceptance, emotional development, perseverance, understanding feelings, and early mathematics skills

Vocabulary

extreme, slightly, mope

Discussion Prompts

- Why do you think the Love Monster feels different from others?
- What does the Love Monster do to try to find someone who loves him?
- Why do you think it was hard for the Love Monster to find love?
- What are some of the places the Love Monster looked for love?
- What happened to the Love Monster at the end of the story?
- How do you think the Love Monster felt when love found him?
- Why is it important to love others just the way they are?
- What does this story teach us about love?
- How would you help the Love Monster if he was your friend?
- What makes the Love Monster special?

Extension Activity

Get ready to bring the Love Monster into your classroom with a hands-on craftivity. Students will create their very own Love Monster, exercising their fine motor skills as they cut, color, and glue different pieces to bring their unique monster to life. This activity not only complements the story's theme of acceptance and love but also allows students to express their creativity and individuality.

At-Home Extension

This interactive activity aims to foster a sense of empathy, creativity, and understanding of diversity, inspired by the themes presented in *Love Monster*.

Materials Needed:
- Paper
- Coloring materials
- Scissors
- Glue or tape
- Googly eyes (optional)
- Other decorative items (stickers, fabric scraps, etc.)

Instructions:

Discuss the Story:
- Begin by discussing *Love Monster* with the child. Focus on how the Love Monster felt different and his journey to find someone who loves him just as he is.
- Talk about the importance of accepting and loving others for their uniqueness.

Designing the Friends:
- Each person (adult and child) will create a "friend" for the Love Monster using paper and cardstock.
- These friends can be monsters or any creature that comes to mind, emphasizing that everyone is unique and special in their own way.

Crafting Together:

- Use the coloring materials to bring the friends to life. Add googly eyes, stickers, or fabric scraps for extra fun.

Storytelling with the New Friends:

- Once the friends are created, engage in a storytelling session.
- Take turns creating stories about these new friends meeting the Love Monster and how they interact, focusing on themes of friendship, acceptance, and love.

Reflection:

- Conclude the activity by reflecting on what each person enjoyed about creating their friend and what they learned about acceptance and kindness.

Owl Moon

by Jane Yolen
Philomel Books ©1987

The Story

Exquisite, detailed illustrations and poetic narrative capture the magic of a nighttime adventure in the woods to spot an elusive owl. This serene and mesmerizing tale celebrates the beauty of nature and the special bond formed through shared experiences. Ideal for quiet read-aloud sessions, it not only captivates with its tranquil storytelling but also introduces children to the wonders of wildlife and the importance of patience and quiet observation. It's a peaceful, enchanting read that beautifully blends a sense of adventure with a deep appreciation for the natural world.

Read-Aloud Tips

Create a Hushed, Whispery Tone: Since the book is set in the quiet of a snowy night, use a soft, whispery voice to reflect the silence and wonder of the setting. This helps create an atmosphere of suspense and awe.

Pause to Appreciate the Illustrations: The book's illustrations are detailed and evocative, capturing the beauty of the winter night. Take your time on each page, allowing the children to absorb the artwork. Point out the subtle details like the shadows, the snow, the trees, and the expressions of the characters.

Emphasize the Sensory Descriptions: Jane Yolen uses rich language to describe the sights, sounds, and sensations of the winter night. Highlight these descriptions to help the children imagine the cold, the sound of snow crunching underfoot, the hooting of the owl, and the stillness of the woods.

Build Suspense: The story is a quiet adventure with a build-up to the appearance of the owl. Use your voice to build suspense and excitement as the child and the father walk through the woods, especially when they stop and listen for the owl.

Discuss the Bond between the Child and the Parent: The story is also about a child sharing a special experience with a parent. Highlight this relationship and ask the children about special experiences they have shared with their family members.

Use Silent Moments Effectively: There are moments in the story where there is no talking, just listening. Use these moments to pause in your reading, emphasizing the quiet of the night and the anticipation of seeing the owl.

Learning Concepts

nature, patience, family bonding, literary devices, sensory experiences, and nocturnal animals

Vocabulary

owling, clearing, threading, meadow

Discussion Prompts

- Who is the narrator?
- How does the narrator feel about going owling with Pa?
- What do you think owling means?
- Why do you think it's important to be quiet when going owling?

- Describe the setting of the story. What does it look like? What does it feel like?
- What does the narrator see and hear during the owling adventure?
- How do the narrator and Pa communicate during their adventure?
- What kind of owl do they see, and how do they find it?
- What do you think the narrator learns from this experience?
- Why do you think the story is called *Owl Moon*?
- What are some words used to describe the night and the snow in the story?
- What is one thing you learned about owls from this story?

Extension Activity

Fly into the world of *Owl Moon* with a hands-on craftivity that not only complements the story but also educates about owls. In this engaging craft, students color, cut, and assemble various parts of an owl, enhancing their fine motor skills while reinforcing their knowledge of this majestic bird. Following the craft, they can also write down facts about owls, integrating art with science and literacy. This activity is a wonderful way to bring the quiet magic of *Owl Moon* to life in your classroom.

At-Home Extension

Inspired by the story *Owl Moon*, this activity aims to connect children with nature through a guided nighttime walk.

Materials Needed:
- Flashlights
- Warm clothing appropriate for the weather
- Binoculars (optional)
- Notebook and pen for observations

Instructions:

Pre-Walk Discussion:
- Begin by talking about the night adventure in *Owl Moon* and discuss the different kinds of nocturnal animals that might be living in your area.

- Go over safety guidelines for being outdoors at night and the importance of staying quiet to observe wildlife.

Selecting a Location:
- Plan your nighttime nature walk in a safe, quiet outdoor area like a local park, forest, or nature trail where nocturnal wildlife is often observed.

Embarking on the Exploration:
- Dress in appropriate attire for the weather and bring your flashlights. Walk quietly and attentively, tuning in to the sounds and movements of the night.

Observation and Discovery:
- Encourage the child to use their senses to observe their surroundings. Listen for animal sounds, watch for movement, and use binoculars for a closer look if needed.
- Discuss the types of nocturnal animals in your area, their habits, habitats, and roles in the ecosystem.

Documenting the Experience:
- Use the notebook to record your observations. The child can write or draw what they see and hear, making it a memorable learning experience.
- This is also an excellent way to engage in a discussion about local biodiversity and nature conservation.

Post-Walk Reflection:
- After your exploration, reflect on your experiences. Discuss what you observed, how it compares to the story *Owl Moon*, and what was most interesting or surprising.
- Use this opportunity to talk about the importance of preserving natural habitats and respecting wildlife.

Reflecting on the Experience:
- After the walk, discuss what you experienced. Ask the child how they felt about the walk and what they found most interesting.
- You can compare your experience to the story of *Owl Moon* and discuss the similarities and differences.

Last Stop on Market Street

by Matt de la Peña

G.P. Putnam's Sons Books for Young Readers ©2015

The Story

A vivid and heartwarming journey seen through the eyes of a young boy and his grandmother as they travel through the city on a bus. With its vibrant illustrations and rich narrative, the story celebrates urban life, diversity, and finding beauty in everyday moments. Ideal for sparking conversations about gratitude, community, and perspective, this book is not only a joy to read aloud but also a wonderful tool for teaching children about the value of appreciating what they have and the diverse world around them. It's a touching, insightful read that leaves a lasting impression.

Read-Aloud Tips

Characterize CJ and His Nana: Give CJ a curious, sometimes puzzled tone to reflect his youthful inquisitiveness. For Nana, use a warm, wise, and cheerful voice to convey her loving and optimistic perspective.

Highlight the Dialogue: The story is driven by the dialogue between CJ and his Nana. Use different voices for their conversation and emphasize the gentle wisdom in Nana's responses to CJ's many questions.

Discuss the Sights and Sounds: As the bus travels through the city, describe the sights and sounds that CJ experiences. Novel Effect really helps to bring the vividness of city life.

Emphasize the Beauty in the Ordinary: Nana helps CJ see the beauty and fun in their everyday environment. Highlight these moments in the story, and encourage the children to think about how they can find beauty in their everyday surroundings.

Learning Concepts

empathy, volunteering, appreciating differences, literary artistry, inequity

Vocabulary

freckle, patter, sag, lurch, pluck, rhythm, witness, arch, stray

Discussion Prompts

- How does CJ feel about taking the bus in the beginning?
- What are some things CJ sees and hears on the bus?
- How does CJ's mood change from the start to the end of the story?
- Who are some people CJ and Nana meet on the bus?
- Why do you think the author included many different characters on the bus?
- What important lesson does CJ learn from his Nana?
- What does the rainbow at the story's end symbolize?
- How did you feel when CJ discovered beauty in his surroundings?
- What would you have enjoyed most about the bus ride if you were CJ?
- What new things might CJ notice on his next bus ride?

Extension Activity

In this activity, students respond to thought-provoking writing prompts that connect the themes of the story. They'll creatively express their ideas within a bus template, symbolizing the journey of the book's characters and their own journey towards community awareness. This activity is a great way to integrate literacy with civic education and inspire meaningful discussions in your classroom.

At-Home Extension

After reading *The Last Stop on Market Street*, explore the community with your little learner. Explain the importance of volunteering and find a place where you can contribute together.

Materials Needed:
- A notebook or journal
- Internet access

Instructions:

Discussion Time:
- Begin by discussing the story. Ask the child what they liked about CJ's journey and what they learned about the community from the book.

Exploration Planning:
- Sit down together and make a list of different types of places in your community, such as parks, libraries, community centers, animal shelters, soup kitchens, and elderly homes.

Research Volunteer Opportunities:
- Use the internet to find volunteer opportunities at the places listed. Discuss with the child the types of help these places might need and how you both could contribute.

Field Trip:
- Plan a day to visit one or more of these places. It could be a simple tour or attending an event they host. This will give a real-life view of the place and the work they do.

Choose a Place to Volunteer:

- After visiting several places and learning about them, decide together on a place where you both would like to volunteer. Consider the impact, the type of work, and the commitment involved.

Post-Volunteering Reflection:

- Reflect on the volunteering experience. Discuss what was learned, how it felt to help, and the importance of being active in the community.

The Scarecrow
....

by Beth Ferry
HarperCollins ©2019

The Story

A tender and beautifully illustrated story that unfolds the unlikely friendship between a lonely scarecrow and a baby crow. This touching narrative explores themes of kindness, compassion, and the transformative power of friendship. Perfect for read-aloud sessions, the book's lyrical prose and poignant illustrations not only captivate young readers but also convey deep messages about empathy and the joy of helping others. It's a heartwarming read that encourages children to look beyond appearances and find beauty in unexpected places and relationships.

Read-Aloud Tips

Set the Scene Visually: Connect with the story's setting and characters by showing the children the cover of the book and some of the beautiful illustrations inside.

Vocal Modulation: Use a soft, gentle voice when describing the scarecrow's loneliness and a more vibrant, warm tone when the scarecrow and the crow develop their friendship. This contrast will help convey the emotional journey within the story.

Character Voices: Give the scarecrow a deep, slow voice, embodying his steady and constant nature. For the crow, use a higher-pitched, curious tone, reflecting its youth and energy.

Pacing: Take your time with the narrative. This story unfolds over seasons, so let your reading pace reflect the passage of time. In short, slow down with this one.

Facial Expressions and Gestures: Since the scarecrow's face doesn't change much, use your facial expressions to reflect what he might be feeling. For instance, show sadness or loneliness when the crow leaves and happiness when it returns. Have your audience join in, asking them to mimic what the crow might look like at different times in the story.

Highlighting the Seasons: As the story progresses through different seasons, bring these to life. For example, shiver slightly during winter scenes or mimic wiping sweat from your brow in the summer parts.

Learning Concepts

friendship and compassion, figurative language,

Vocabulary

woodland, velvet, bud, lullaby, perch, fledgling, caw, sag, midair, brim, mend, matted

Discussion Prompts

- What is a scarecrow's main job?
- How do the animals initially feel about the scarecrow?
- How does the scarecrow feel when he is alone?
- How does the scarecrow help the crow?

- What changes in the scarecrow after he helps the crow?
- How does the friendship between the scarecrow and the crow make you feel?
- What do you think the scarecrow learns from his friendship with the crow?
- How does the scarecrow feel when the crow leaves?
- What surprises the scarecrow at the end of the story?
- How does the ending of the story make you feel?
- What is the main message or lesson of the story?

Extension Activity

In this engaging craftivity, students bring the story to life by creating a pop-up paper craft. After reading the book, they illustrate scenes from key events and characters, capturing the heartwarming moments between the scarecrow and the animals. As they assemble their pop-up, they develop both artistic skills and a deeper connection to the narrative, making it a hands-on way to reflect on the story's themes.

At-Home Extension

Inspired by the themes of friendship and kindness in *The Scarecrow*, this activity calls for acts of kindness in the community. The goal is to understand the importance of helping others, just as the scarecrow helps the crow in the story.

Materials Needed:
- Paper
- Writing materials

Instructions:

Pre-Activity Discussion:
- Discuss the story *The Scarecrow*, focusing on how the scarecrow's act of kindness changed the life of the crow. Talk about how small acts of kindness can have a big impact.

Creating Kindness Cards:

- Together, create "Kindness Cards." These can be simple cards that say things like "You're appreciated!" or "Have a great day!" Decorate them with drawings or stickers.

Planning Acts of Kindness:

- Make a list of acts of kindness you can do in your community. This might include giving out the Kindness Cards, helping a neighbor with yard work, or donating food to a local pantry.

Kindness Adventure:

- Spend a day or a few hours performing these acts of kindness. Hand out the Kindness Cards, offer help where needed, and engage positively with those you meet.

Reflection:

- Encourage the child to write or draw a story about their experience, imagining how their acts of kindness might have positively affected those around them, similar to the scarecrow's impact in the story.

The Invisible String

by Patrice Karst
Little, Brown Books for Young Readers ©2018

The Story

A comforting and imaginative story that explores the invisible but unbreakable connections of love between people, no matter the distance. With its gentle narrative and soothing illustrations, it addresses the complex feelings of loneliness and separation, offering a reassuring message of love's enduring presence. Ideal for read-aloud sessions, especially in times of change or absence, this book not only provides emotional support but also sparks discussions about relationships, emotions, and the invisible ties that bind us. It's a heartening read that resonates with both children and adults, offering a sense of security and connection.

Read-Aloud Tips

Introduction: Start by explaining the concept of the invisible string in simple terms. The idea is abstract and building some background knowledge and understanding before the story begins is key.

Tone and Pacing: Use a soothing, gentle tone to match the comforting nature of the story. The pacing should be slow and deliberate, allowing the listeners to absorb the concept and the emotions that come with it.

Character Voices: For the mother, use a calm, reassuring tone. For Liza and Jeremy, a curious and inquisitive voice will convey their initial fear and eventual understanding and comfort.

Have Tissues: Especially with the Novel Effect soundscape, this story really hits home. Be prepared, both for yourself and your audience, with a box of tissues nearby.

Learning Concepts

Loss, resilience, dealing with fear and anxiety, community, spirituality

Vocabulary

invisible, rumble, tug, submarine

Discussion Prompts

- What do you think the "invisible string" represents in the story?
- Can you think of a time when you felt connected to someone even when they weren't with you?
- How can we feel the invisible string in our hearts?
- What are some ways you show love to people you are connected to with your invisible string?
- Do you think animals, like Jasper the cat, have invisible strings too? Why or why not?
- What does the story teach us about love and being connected to others?
- Think of someone your invisible string is connected to who is far away.
- How does the invisible string stay strong even when we are angry or upset with someone?

- Why do you think the invisible string doesn't go away as we grow older?
- What are some ways we can keep our invisible strings strong with people we care about?

Extension Activity

This activity complements the themes presented in *The Invisible String*. Students are encouraged to draw and write about four people they feel a deep connection with, symbolizing their own invisible strings. This activity helps children understand and express the concept of emotional bonds and the idea that we are always connected to those we love, regardless of physical distance.

At-Home Extension

Visually represent connections within your family or community using string to symbolize the "invisible strings" of love and care.

Materials Needed:
- A ball of string or yarn
- Scissors
- A large poster board or a corkboard
- Pushpins (if using a corkboard) or tape (if using a poster board)
- Markers or pens
- Small paper tags or sticky notes

Instructions:

Preparation:
- Set up the poster board or corkboard in a common area where the family can gather around.

Introduction:
- Explain to the child that each family member is connected by invisible strings of love, just like in the story. This activity will create a visual representation of those connections.

Personal Tags:

• Start by giving each family member a paper tag or sticky note. Ask them to write their name on it and attach it to the board using a pushpin or tape.

Creating Connections:

• Take the ball of string and cut a piece to connect the first two family members. Tie or tape one end to the first person's tag and extend it to the second person's tag, securing it in place. As you do this, encourage the family to share how they feel connected to each other, discussing times they felt the "invisible string" tug at their hearts.

Continue the Web:

• Repeat this process, connecting each family member's tag with multiple strings, forming a web. Encourage discussions about different types of connections, such as shared interests, moments of support, or shared experiences.

Reflection:

• Once the web is complete, stand back and observe. Reflect on how intertwined and connected everyone is. Discuss how, like the strings, family bonds remain strong and supportive, even when not physically together.

Maintenance:

• Leave the web on display as a reminder of family connections. Family members can add new strings or tags as the family grows or as new significant connections are formed.

The Adventures of Beekle: The Unimaginary Friend

By Dan Santat

Little, Brown Books for Young Readers ©2014

The Story

A whimsical and heartwarming tale of an imaginary friend waiting to be chosen by a child. With its imaginative storyline and charming illustrations, the book captures the magic of friendship and the power of believing in the unseen. Perfect for sparking creativity and discussions about friendship and imagination, this story not only delights with its unique premise but also teaches important lessons about patience, persistence, and the joy of finding one's perfect match. It's a delightful and uplifting read that encourages children to embrace the unseen world of imagination and the value of true friendship.

Read-Aloud Tips

Set a Magical Tone: Begin by setting the stage for a world of imagination. Use a soft, whimsical voice to introduce Beekle and the magical land where imaginary friends wait to be chosen by children.

Characterize Beekle: Give Beekle a curious, hopeful voice to reflect his patience and longing. As he ventures into the real world, gradually add excitement and determination to his voice to show his persistence and bravery.

Use Expressive Pauses: When Beekle waits or feels unsure, pause slightly to build anticipation. Let children feel his emotions during key moments of waiting or self-doubt.

Highlight the Contrast: Emphasize the difference between the colorful, imaginative world and the gray, ordinary real world. Change your tone and pacing when describing the real world to reflect Beekle's sense of unfamiliarity.

Engage with Questions: Throughout the story, ask questions to spark imagination, such as "What kind of imaginary friend would you want?" or "Why do you think Beekle feels different?"

Capture Beekle's Emotions: When Beekle finally meets his friend, use an uplifting, joyful tone to capture the magic of the moment. Show excitement and relief as Beekle's journey comes to a heartwarming end.

Learning Concepts

Friendship, courage and bravery, empathy, problem-solving

Vocabulary

imaginary, eager, courage, journey, familiar, unimaginable

Discussion Prompts

- How do you think Beekle felt when he was waiting to be chosen by a child? Have you ever felt like that?
- Beekle did something unimaginable by sailing to the real world. Have you ever done something brave when you were scared?
- When Beekle arrived in the real world, everything was different. How do you feel when you go somewhere new?

- Describe a time when you made a new friend. How did it happen? Was it similar to how Beekle found his friend?
- How do you think having Beekle changed Alice's life?
- Why do you think Beekle and Alice were a perfect match? What makes someone a good friend?
- Imagine you are an imaginary friend like Beekle. What child would you like to be friends with, and why?
- What did you learn about friendship from Beekle's story?
- Write a short story about an adventure you and your imaginary friend would have together.

Extension Activity

In this creative exercise, students will tap into their imagination and artistic skills. They will be tasked with drawing and describing their own unique imaginary character, encouraging them to explore their creativity and storytelling abilities. This activity not only fosters artistic expression but also aids in developing their descriptive writing and cognitive skills.

At-Home Extension

This shared creative exercise encourages imagination, storytelling, and artistic expression.

Materials Needed:
- Drawing paper
- Coloring materials
- Scissors
- Glue

Instructions:

Discussion:
- Start by discussing the story of Beekle. Ask your child questions about the book, such as their favorite parts, how they felt about Beekle's journey, and what they think about imaginary friends.

Create Your Imaginary Friend:

- Each of you (parent and child) should draw your own imaginary friend. This can be inspired by Beekle or entirely unique. Discuss the features of your imaginary friends as you draw them. Give them names and special abilities.

Design an Imaginary World:

- On a large piece of paper, work together to create a world for these imaginary friends. This could be a magical forest, a colorful city, or a mysterious planet. Encourage your child to let their imagination run wild.

Storytelling:

- Once the world is created, make up stories about what adventures your imaginary friends might have in this world. Take turns adding elements to the story, building on each other's ideas.

Crafting (Optional):

- If you have craft supplies, you can add a 3D element to your world. Use scissors and glue to create layered effects or add decorative elements like glitter or stickers for a more immersive experience.

Giraffes Can't Dance
....

By Giles Andreae
Cartwheel Books ©2012

The Story

An inspiring and colorfully illustrated story about a giraffe who, despite initial doubts, discovers his own unique way of dancing. It's a wonderful tale that encourages children to embrace their individuality and find their own rhythm in life. This book not only entertains with its vibrant jungle setting and engaging narrative but also imparts important lessons about self-confidence, perseverance, and the beauty of being different. It's a joyful and uplifting read that motivates young readers to dance to the beat of their own drum.

Read-Aloud Tips

Use Expressive Voices: The book features a variety of animals, each with its own personality. Give the lions a deep, growly voice and the crickets a high, squeaky tone.

Highlight Gerald's Emotions: Gerald, the giraffe, goes through a range of emotions–from sadness and embarrassment to joy and confidence. Use your voice to express these emotions, sounding a bit downcast when Gerald feels left out and bright and cheerful as he discovers his own way of dancing.

Engage with the Illustrations: The book is known for its vibrant and colorful illustrations. Spend time on each page, pointing out the details in the pictures. Ask the children to describe what they see and how the images make them feel.

The Jungle Dance: Since the book is about dancing, encourage the children to stand up and dance throughout the story, and especially at the Jungle Dance.

Soundscape Is a Must: This might be one of the best soundscapes in all of Novel Effect, where every child will be swaying with the music. Hearing the different music at the Jungle Dance and the cricket's song truly bring this story to life.

Learning Concepts

Self-esteem, kindness, embracing unique talents, acceptance

Vocabulary

slim, crooked, munch, shoots, buckle, prance, waltz, tango, splendid, reel, clumsy, sneer, root, clot, sway

Discussion Prompts

- How did Gerald the giraffe feel when he couldn't dance at the Jungle Dance?
- Have you ever felt like Gerald, worried about not being able to do something well? How did you handle it?
- How did the cricket help Gerald feel better?
- How did Gerald's feelings change from the beginning to the end of the story?
- Can you think of a time when someone encouraged you, like the cricket encouraged Gerald?
- How did Gerald find his own way to dance in the end?
- If you were Gerald, what would you have done when the animals laughed at you?

- What kind of dance would you like to try, and why?
- Why is it important to believe in yourself, like Gerald did?
- How can we help others who might feel sad or left out, just like Gerald felt?
- What does this story teach us about being different?
- What do you think is the message or lesson of this story?

Extension Activity

Students express their creativity by coloring a giraffe and responding to a thought-provoking prompt related to the book, encouraging them to reflect on the themes of individuality, perseverance, and growth mindset. Once completed, these colorful giraffes can be cut out and used on a bulletin board or growth mindset display.

At-Home Extension

Explore different music styles with your little learner and express personality through dance, while also sharing and discussing your cultural heritage.

Materials Needed:
- A phone, computer, or tablet to access music
- A comfortable, open space for dancing

Instructions:

Introduction:
- Sit together and briefly discuss the story of *Giraffes Can't Dance*. Talk about how Gerald found his own unique way to dance and how every type of music made him feel differently.

Music Selection (Parent):
- Prepare a playlist that includes a variety of music styles mentioned in the book, as well as a few tracks that are culturally significant to your family. Explain to your child the origin or significance of each piece of music, especially those from your own culture.

Dance Time:

- Play each track one by one. Encourage your child to dance freely to each type of music, expressing how the music makes them feel.

Role Reversal (Optional):

- If the child is able, they can choose a song and ask the parent to dance, demonstrating their own moves.

Discussion:

- After dancing to all the music, sit down and discuss the experience. Ask your child which type of music they liked best and why. Share your own feelings about the music and dances you both did.

Reflection:

- Finally, talk about the importance of celebrating differences and finding one's own rhythm in life, just like Gerald did in the story.

We Will Rock Our Classmates

by Ryan T. Higgins
Disney Hyperion ©2020

The Story

An empowering and lively story about a young dinosaur who overcomes her fears to share her passion for music with her classmates. With vibrant illustrations and a relatable narrative, the book captures the excitement and nerves of expressing oneself. Perfect for classroom read-alouds, it not only entertains with its fun storyline but also teaches important lessons about self-expression, courage, and the supportiveness of friends. It's an inspiring and enjoyable read that encourages children to embrace their talents and share their unique interests with others.

Read-Aloud Tips

Highlight Penelope's Character: Penelope is a unique character—a dinosaur among human classmates. Emphasize her distinctness and the emotions she experiences. Use a voice that reflects her nervousness and excitement, helping children connect with her character.

Play with Voice Modulations: As Penelope is the only dinosaur in her class, use a slightly different voice for her compared to the human characters. This distinction will help young listeners easily identify when Penelope is speaking or the focus of the story.

Encourage Participation: During the talent show scenes, encourage the children to pretend they are part of the audience. They can clap, cheer, and react to Penelope's performance, making the reading more interactive.

Use Humor: The book has humorous elements, especially involving Penelope and a pony in the talent show. Use a playful and light-hearted tone to bring out this humor.

Learning Concepts

courage, self-expression, positive thinking

Vocabulary

stand out, talent, ferocious, concert, rehearsal, supper, album, marathon, nerve, courage, synchronized, dazzling

Discussion Prompts

- What is the main character's name, and what makes her special?
- Why was Penelope nervous about the school talent show?
- What kind of music does Penelope love to play and sing?
- Can you think of a time when you felt different like Penelope? How did you feel?
- How did Penelope's parents encourage her when she was feeling down?
- What made Penelope decide to sign up for the talent show?
- How did Penelope's dad help her feel better about being in the talent show?

- What did Penelope's classmates do to show their support?
- How did Penelope feel right before her performance?
- What did Penelope learn about herself and her abilities by the end of the book?
- If you were in Penelope's school, would you like to be in her band? Why or why not?

Extension Activity

Students will build their own paper guitar to complement the book *We Will Rock Our Classmates*. Inside each guitar, students will respond to writing prompts related to the story. This multifaceted activity not only reinforces their understanding of the book but also allows them to connect with the story in a unique and artistic way.

At-Home Extension

After reading *We Will Rock Our Classmates*, engage in a fun and interactive activity by organizing a talent show at home. This activity not only provides a fun family bonding experience but also encourages each family member to express themselves creatively, just like Penelope in the book. It's a great way to celebrate individual talents and create lasting memories together.

Planning the Talent Show:
- Gather as a family and decide on a day and time for your talent show. It could be on a weekend evening when everyone can relax and enjoy the performances.

Choosing Talents:
- Each family member gets to choose a talent or skill they would like to showcase. It could be anything from singing, dancing, playing an instrument, or reciting a poem, to performing a magic trick, or even a comedy routine.

Preparation Time:
- Allocate some time for each family member to prepare for their performance. This could involve practicing a song, choreographing a dance, or preparing any props needed.

Setting the Stage:

- Create a performance area in your living room or any spacious part of your house. Arrange seating for the audience (family members who are not performing) and a "stage" area for the performances.

The Big Night:

- On the day of the talent show, everyone dresses up as if they were going to a real talent show. Create a program listing the order of performances.

Performance Time:

- Let each family member take turns performing their talent. Make sure to cheer and applaud for each performer, showing support and appreciation.

Celebration:

- After everyone has performed, celebrate with a special treat like ice cream or a favorite family dessert. Discuss what everyone enjoyed about the talent.

The Bad Seed

By Jory John
HarperCollins ©2017

The Story

A witty and insightful story about a seed who has a reputation for being "bad," but who decides to make a change for the better. With its humorous narrative and expressive illustrations, the book offers a fresh perspective on behavior, choices, and the possibility of change. Ideal for discussions about emotions and actions, this story not only entertains with its unique character but also imparts important lessons about self-awareness, the power of intention, and the journey of personal growth. It's a delightful read that combines humor with meaningful life lessons.

Read-Aloud Tips

Repetition: The book frequently uses the phrase "baaaaaad seed" to emphasize the character's bad behavior. Emphasize this repetition when reading aloud to create a rhythm and help children remember the key theme of the book.

Use Expressive Voice for Character Development: The seed goes through a significant transformation from being bad to trying to be good. Reflect this change in your tone of voice, starting with a grumpy, mischievous tone and gradually shifting to a more cheerful and hopeful one as the seed changes.

Highlight the Seed's Emotions: Throughout the story, the seed experiences a range of emotions which can be conveyed in your tone.

- Frustration or Anger: A slightly louder, brisk tone can convey the seed's initial bad behavior.
- Sadness or Remorse: A softer, slower, and lower tone can express the seed's regret and sadness.
- Hope or Happiness: As the seed decides to change, use a brighter, more energetic tone to show its newfound optimism.

Emphasize the Moral: Highlight the transformation of the seed from bad to good. Stress the importance of not judging others and the power of change and redemption. This can be a gentle way to teach children about empathy and personal growth.

Learning Concepts

self-awareness, empathy, character development and transformation, problem-solving

Vocabulary

mumble, pointless, humble, unremarkable, droop, holler, drift, suit

Discussion Prompts

- What are some of the bad things the Bad Seed did? Why do you think he did them?
- The Bad Seed used to be on a sunflower. How do you think he felt when he was part of the sunflower?

- What happened to the Bad Seed that made him change and start acting badly?
- The Bad Seed decided he didn't want to be bad anymore. What made him want to change?
- What are some good things the Bad Seed started doing to change his behavior?
- Why do you think it's hard for the Bad Seed to be good sometimes?
- What does this story teach us about how we treat others who might seem different?
- What does the story tell us about making mistakes and learning from them?
- How important is it to say "please" and "thank you" like the Bad Seed learned to do?
- If you were a friend of the Bad Seed, how would you help him feel better?
- What is the main message or lesson of *The Bad Seed*?

Extension Activity

This activity is a hands-on approach for students to explore and understand the themes of the book.

Through sorting good and bad traits and choices, students will engage in critical thinking about behavior and its consequences. This exercise not only reinforces the book's messages about personal growth and accountability but also encourages students to reflect on their own actions and choices. This activity is ideal for fostering discussions on character development, decision-making, and empathy in a classroom setting.

At-Home Extension

This activity provides a hands-on gardening experience and also serves as a metaphor for growth and acceptance. Reinforce the positive message from *The Bad Seed* and encourage ongoing discussions about personal development and empathy with your little learner.

Materials Needed:
- A variety of seeds (flowers, vegetables, or easy-to-grow plants)
- Small pots or a garden patch
- Soil
- Gardening tools (optional)
- Colored markers and stickers
- Paper and pencils

Instructions:

Discussion:
- Start with a conversation about the book. Ask your child how they think the Bad Seed felt when he was not accepted and how he felt when he decided to change. Discuss the importance of acceptance and comfort in both the garden and in life.

Creating the Comfort Garden:
- Each choose a seed or a set of seeds. Explain that just like in the story, every seed, regardless of its type, has the potential to grow into something beautiful.

Decorating the Pots:
- Use markers and/or stickers to decorate the pots. Encourage your child to draw symbols of comfort and acceptance—like hearts, smiling faces, or suns.

Planting the Seeds:
- Plant the seeds together in the decorated pots. While planting, discuss how every seed needs care, comfort, and acceptance to grow, just like people do.

Daily Care:
- Assign the responsibility of watering and caring for the plant to your child, explaining that nurturing and accepting the plant will help it grow.

Reflection Time:
- Once the activity is over, discuss what you both learned from this activity. Focus on themes like growth, change, and acceptance.

Regular Check-ins:
- Regularly check on the growth of your plants together. Use these moments to reflect on personal growth and changes, emphasizing that, like the plants, we all need comfort and acceptance to thrive.

Be Who You Are

by Todd Parr
Little, Brown Books for Young Readers ©2016

The Story

A vibrant and affirming story that celebrates the joy and freedom of being true to oneself. With its colorful illustrations and uplifting narrative, the book encourages children to embrace their individuality, from their appearance to their interests and beliefs. This story not only entertains but also fosters important conversations about diversity, self-acceptance, and the beauty of uniqueness. It's an inspiring and joyful read that empowers young readers to confidently express their true selves in all their wonderful diversity.

Read-Aloud Tips

Maintain a Joyful, Playful Tone: The book's style is fun and lighthearted. Maintain a joyful, playful tone throughout the reading to match the book's spirit. This approach will help convey its uplifting message effectively.

Emphasize Self-Acceptance and Diversity: The book's central theme is about being proud of who you are. When reading, emphasize this message by using a warm, affirmative tone. Highlight sentences that focus on individuality, such as "Be proud of where you're from" or "Be a different color. Speak your language." This will reinforce the book's positive message.

Learning Concepts

individuality, self-acceptance, celebrating diversity, confidence

Vocabulary

different, language, proud, discover, confident, energetic, yoga

Discussion Prompts

- What does it mean to "be who you are"?
- Name three ways you are different from your friends.
- What is your favorite thing about yourself?
- Why is it important to love others for who they are?
- What are some ways you can show kindness to someone?
- How do you feel when you try something new?
- What is one new thing you would like to try?
- What foods do you love that are part of your family's culture?
- How can you be a good friend to someone who is feeling sad or scared?
- What are some things you do when you feel happy, sad, or angry?
- What does being brave mean to you?
- Why is it good to share your feelings with others?
- How do you show love to yourself and others?

Extension Activity

Have your students celebrate their individuality and share what makes them special. Encourage students to express themselves through writing or drawing, highlighting their personal interests, talents, and qualities. This activity not only fosters a sense of self-awareness and confidence among students but also nurtures an environment of respect and appreciation for diversity in the classroom.

At-Home Extension

Celebrate individuality by creating a collage with your little learner!

Materials Needed:
- Blank paper
- Coloring supplies
- Magazines, old newspapers (for cutting out images)
- Glue or tape

Instructions:

Reflection Time:
- Start by sitting together with the book *Be Who You Are*. Ask your child what makes them special, and what they love about themself.

Collage:
- You and your little learner will cut images or words from magazines to create collages that represent each of you.
- This could include your favorite things, dreams, what makes you happy, your favorite foods, places you love, or activities you enjoy.

Share and Appreciate:
- Once you both have finished your artwork, take turns to share your unique worlds with each other. Discuss the similarities and differences with joy and appreciation, highlighting the beauty in diversity.

Display Your Art:
- Find a place in your home to display your artworks, as a reminder of this special bonding activity and the uniqueness of each family member.

What Do You Do with an Idea?

by Kobi Yamada
Compendium, Inc. ©2014

The Story

A thought-provoking and beautifully illustrated story about a child who nurtures a fledgling idea into something extraordinary. This inspiring tale encourages young readers to embrace their creativity and the possibilities that come with it. This book not only captivates with its whimsical art but also imparts important messages about perseverance, the power of innovation, and the courage to bring one's ideas to life. It's an uplifting read that celebrates the journey of an idea and its potential to change the world.

Read-Aloud Tips

Highlight the Growth of the Idea: The story follows an idea that grows as the child's confidence increases. Emphasize this progression by changing your tone and volume as the idea develops. Start with a softer, more curious tone and gradually become more assertive and confident as the idea takes shape.

Create a Supportive Atmosphere: The book is about nurturing an idea despite doubts and fears. Create a supportive atmosphere during the reading by affirming the children's thoughts and ideas, showing them that just like in the story, their ideas are valuable and worth exploring.

Engage with the Illustrations: The illustrations by Mae Besom play a crucial role in the story. They start with muted tones with the idea depicted in a striking orangey-gold color. As you read, point out how the idea (and the colors in the illustrations) grow and become more vibrant. This visual change mirrors the narrative and helps children understand the growth of the idea.

Learning Concepts

nature of ideas, creative process, entrepreneurship, confidence

Vocabulary

fragile, attention

Discussion Prompts

- What did the child first think about the idea when it appeared?
- How did the child feel when they walked away from the idea?
- Why did the child decide to keep the idea a secret?
- How did the idea grow as the child took care of it?
- What were some of the reactions of other people when they saw the idea?
- Why did the child decide not to give up on the idea?
- How did the child protect and care for the idea?
- What special house did the child build for the idea?
- How did the idea encourage the child to think differently?

- What amazing change happened to the idea one day?
- How did the idea transform from being part of the child to being part of everything?
- What did the child realize is the most important thing to do with an idea?

Extension Activity

Inspired by the book *What Do You Do with an Idea?* students are encouraged to explore their imagination by sketching an idea that is special to them, much like the child in the story. They then write a short piece about their idea to foster creativity, self-expression, and a deeper understanding of the value and potential of their own ideas.

At-Home Extension

Help your little learner foster planning skills, problem-solving, and the value of perseverance by creating an idea roadmap together.

Materials Needed:
- Paper
- Coloring materials

Instructions:

Idea Reflection and Selection:
- Start by discussing the key message of *What Do You Do with an Idea?* and encourage the child to think of an idea they are passionate about. This could be anything from a small project, like a garden or a craft, to a bigger concept like helping others in their community.

Creating the Idea Journey Map:
- Using a sheet of paper or poster board, guide the child to draw a map that outlines the steps they think they need to take to make their idea a reality. Begin with where the idea is currently (just a thought) and end with the idea being fully realized.

Identify Key Steps and Milestones:

- Together, brainstorm and identify key steps needed to bring the idea to life. This might include gathering materials, learning new skills, asking for help from adults or friends, or any other steps relevant to their specific idea.

Overcoming Obstacles:

- Include potential challenges or obstacles on the map and discuss ways to overcome them. This encourages problem-solving skills and resilience.

Plan of Action:

- Next to each step on the map, leave space for notes or action items. This transforms the map into a working plan that the child can follow.

Regular Check-ins and Updates:

- Finally, plan regular check-ins to discuss progress on the map, update it as necessary, and celebrate achievements along the way. This reinforces the idea that bringing an idea to life is a journey with evolving steps.

The Dot

....

by Peter Reynolds
Candlewick ©2003

The Story

The Dot tells a story of a clever art teacher who challenges a student to overcome self-doubt and "make her mark." It begins with just a small dot on a piece of paper. That dot sparks Vashti to make more dots, bigger dots, colored dots, and more. This read-aloud is a MUST for every child and will challenge listeners to conquer their fears one dot at a time, put themselves out there, and create!

Read-Aloud Tips

Emphasize the Power of Encouragement: Use a gentle, encouraging tone when voicing the art teacher, showing how positive words can spark transformation in Vashti. Highlight the kindness and belief the teacher has in Vashti's potential.

Build on Vashti's Journey: Begin with a reluctant, uncertain tone for Vashti, but as the story progresses, add more confidence and energy to her voice, reflecting her growing self-belief.

Use Dramatic Pauses: When Vashti first makes her dot, pause for a moment to let the children absorb the importance of that small act. Let them feel how something seemingly insignificant can become meaningful.

Invite Participation: Ask the listeners to imagine themselves in Vashti's place. "What would your first dot look like?" or "How would you feel if someone didn't believe in your art?"

Learning Concepts

Creativity, self-confidence, growth mindset, art

Vocabulary

jab, experiment, gaze

Discussion Prompts

- How did Vashti make her first mark on the paper?
- What did Vashti's teacher do with the paper after Vashti made her mark?
- What happened at the school art show with Vashti's dots?
- What did the little boy at the art show say to Vashti?
- How did Vashti encourage the boy who said he couldn't draw?
- What did Vashti tell the boy to do with his drawing?
- How did you feel when you saw how Vashti's confidence grew throughout the story?
- How do you think encouragement from others, like Vashti's teacher, can help us?
- What do you think the story teaches us about making mistakes and trying again?
- How did Vashti's attitude change from the beginning to the end of the book?
- What do you think is the message of the story?
- How do you feel about trying new things after reading about Vashti's journey?

Extension Activity

This activity based on the book *The Dot* is designed to encourage creativity and self-expression. Each student will create their own unique dot artwork and sign it, mirroring Vashti's journey in the story. After the students complete their dots, assemble all the framed artworks into a student art gallery. This gallery not only showcases their artistic talents but also serves as a beautiful reminder of the power of encouragement and the joy of trying something new.

At-Home Extension

Encourage imagination, art, and storytelling, inspired by the creative journey in *The Dot*.

Materials Needed:
- Paper
- Tape or glue
- Coloring supplies

Instructions:

Set the Scene:
- After reading *The Dot*, discuss how a simple dot can lead to a big adventure. Explain that you'll both create a continuous story using only dots and simple shapes.

Create Your Canvas:
- Connect several sheets to make a long, continuous canvas.

Start the Story:
- The adult begins by placing a dot or a simple shape anywhere on the paper. As you do this, start a story based on this shape. For example, "This red dot is a brave ladybug starting her journey."

Child's Turn:
- The child then adds their dot or shape, continuing the story. Encourage them to build on the narrative you started or take it in a new direction.

Keep Adding:

- Take turns adding dots and shapes, each time elaborating on the story. Use different colors, sizes, and tools (like the edge of a coin or a stamp pad) to make your marks.

Finalize Your Story:

- Once your canvas is filled, or you feel the story has come to a natural end, take a moment to retell the entire story from start to finish, pointing out each part on your canvas.

Rosie Revere, Engineer

by Andrea Beaty

Harry N. Abrams ©2013

The Story

An inspiring and delightfully illustrated story about a young girl with a passion for inventing. Rosie's journey of overcoming fear of failure and realizing that every "failure" is a step towards success resonates powerfully with readers. Ideal for encouraging STEM interest in children, this book not only entertains with its inventive storyline and engaging characters but also teaches important lessons about perseverance, creativity, and the value of learning from mistakes. It's a motivating read that empowers young minds to explore, invent, and believe in their own abilities to create and succeed.

Read-Aloud Tips

Character Voices:

- Rosie: Portray Rosie with a voice that reflects her shy yet imaginative and determined nature. When she's inventing, use a more excited and energetic tone. After her invention fails and she feels discouraged, use a softer, more with-drawn tone. As she gains confidence, gradually bring back the energy and excitement in your voice.

- Great-Great-Aunt Rose: Give her a spirited and encourag-ing voice, highlighting her role as a mentor and source of inspiration for Rosie. Emphasize the wisdom and kindness in her voice, especially when she teaches Rosie about the importance of perseverance.

Pacing and Emotion: The story has ups and downs, reflect-ing Rosie's emotional journey. Read slowly and thoughtfully during the more introspective moments, especially when Rosie feels defeated. Speed up your reading when Rosie is busy inventing, to convey her enthusiasm and creativity. Use pauses effectively when Rosie learns from her failures.

Learning Concepts

STEM, growth mindset, problem-solving, cause and effect, creativity

Vocabulary

engineer, stash, eaves, gizmo, perplex, dismay, relation, linger, haul, sputter, lever, baffle, perplex

Discussion Prompts

- What kind of gadgets and gizmos did Rosie make in her attic?
- Why did Rosie hide her machines under her bed?
- How did Rosie feel when her Uncle Fred laughed at her cheese hat invention?
- Why did Rosie decide to keep her dreams to herself after Uncle Fred's reaction?
- How did Rosie react to her aunt's wish to fly?
- What was Rosie's plan to help her aunt fly?
- How did Rosie's cheesecopter invention perform during its test flight?

- What was Rosie's reaction to the cheesecopter crashing?
- How did Great-Great-Aunt Rose encourage Rosie after the cheesecopter crashed?
- What important lesson did Rosie learn about failure and being an engineer?
- How can you apply this story's lesson to your future endeavors?

Extension Activity

Let students explore their creativity and problem-solving skills by planning and designing their own unique inventions. Through sketching and responding to thought-provoking prompts, students will deepen their understanding of the engineering process. This exercise is a fun way to integrate art and science and foster a spirit of inquiry among your students.

At-Home Extension

Encourage creativity, problem-solving, and teamwork with this fun Inventor's Workshop activity!

Materials Needed:
- Recycled materials
- Tape or glue
- Coloring supplies (optional)

Instructions:

Discussion:
- Start by discussing the story of *Rosie Revere, Engineer*. Ask the child what they liked about Rosie's inventions and what they learned about trying, failing, and persevering.

Idea Brainstorming:
- Together, brainstorm ideas for an invention. It could be something useful, something fun, or even something wacky! Discuss what problem the invention might solve or what purpose it serves.

Sketch the Invention:

- Use paper and pencils to sketch the proposed invention.

Gather Materials:

- Look around the house for materials that can be used to build a replica of the invention. Remember, like Rosie, you can use recyclable materials!

Build Time:

- Work together to build the invention. This is where creativity and problem-solving come into play. If something doesn't work as expected, encourage the child to think of new ways to solve the problem, just like Rosie did.

Share Your Invention:

- Once your replica is complete, take turns explaining how it works. Discuss what was challenging about building it and what you both learned in the process.

Reflect:

- Conclude by reflecting on the activity. Ask questions like, "What was your favorite part of building the invention?" and "What would you do differently next time?"

Mae Among the Stars

by Roda Ahmed
HarperCollins ©2018

The Story

An inspiring and beautifully illustrated story based on the life of Mae Jemison, the first African American woman astronaut. This heartwarming tale encourages young readers to dream big and work hard to achieve their goals. The narrative, filled with wonder and determination, is perfect for discussions about aspirations, perseverance, and the importance of support from loved ones. It's not only a celebration of Mae Jemison's achievements but also a powerful message to children that with belief and dedication, the sky's the limit for their dreams.

Read-Aloud Tips

Set the Stage: Before reading, ask the children what they want to be when they grow up so there is a more personal connection to the story.

Voicing Mae: Portray Mae with a voice filled with wonder and curiosity, especially when she talks about space and her dreams. This will help convey her passion and determination. When Mae faces discouragement, such as from her teacher, slightly alter your tone to reflect her disappointment, but maintain an underlying sense of hope and resilience.

Narration Tone: Use a tone of admiration and inspiration when narrating the story, to reflect the awe-inspiring nature of Mae's journey and achievements. Adjust your tone, being more upbeat and enthusiastic when Mae is excited about her dreams, and more somber when she faces setbacks.

Learning Concepts

Space, goal setting, perseverance

Vocabulary

daydreamer, astronaut, crystal, profession

Discussion Prompts

- What did Mae dream about becoming when she grew up?
- How did Mae show her interest in space at home?
- What was Mae's concern about becoming an astronaut, and how did her dad respond?
- Describe the dream Mae had about space. How did it make her feel?
- When Mae shared her dream in class, how did the other children react? Why do you think they reacted that way?
- How did Miss Bell, the teacher, react to Mae's dream? Did you agree with her reaction?
- What advice did Mae's mom give her when she was upset about what her teacher said?
- Do you think it's important to follow your dreams, even when others don't believe in them? Why or why not?
- How did Mae prove to everyone that she could achieve her dream?
- If you were Mae, how would you feel looking at Earth from space?

- What is one dream you have for the future, and what can you do now to start working towards it?
- Would you want to be an astronaut? Why or why not?

Extension Activity

Soar further into the inspiring story of *Mae Among the Stars*. The first part of the activity involves sequencing: students cut and paste events in the correct order, enhancing their understanding of the story's progression and reinforcing key plot points. In the second part, students will reflect on the emotional journey of Mae. This activity strengthens comprehension skills and encourages students to think critically about the emotional development of characters.

At-Home Extension

Ask your young dreamer, just like Mae, to think of a space or Earth job they'd love to have one day. Dreamers should gather five items from around the room that remind them of this cosmic career. They can also illustrate pictures if resources relating to their dream job are limited. After collecting the items, see if you can guess their dream job based on their out-of-this-world choices!

The Most Magnificent Thing

by Ashley Spires
Kids Can Press ©2014

The Story

A creatively illustrated and engaging story about a girl and her dog who set out to make the most magnificent thing. The journey of their project, filled with trials, frustrations, and eventual success, beautifully illustrates the creative process. This book not only entertains with its relatable narrative and charming characters but also teaches important lessons about perseverance, the value of taking breaks, and the joy of bringing a vision to life. It's an inspiring and enjoyable read that encourages young readers to embrace creativity, problem-solving, and the understanding that sometimes, the path to success involves a few setbacks.

Read-Aloud Tips

Characters:
- The Girl: Give her a voice that is full of determination and enthusiasm, especially when she first sets out to create her magnificent thing. As she encounters challenges, let her voice reflect her growing frustration and disappointment.

- Narration: Use a clear and expressive voice to narrate the story, emphasizing the ups and downs of the girl's creative process.

Expressing Emotions: The story is rich in emotional content. Use a quicker and more excited voice as she starts building, and slower and more subdued as she becomes frustrated. When the girl has her outburst, increase your volume slightly to convey her anger, then gradually soften your voice as she calms down during her walk.

Important Pauses: Use a long pause after the girl's creation breaks, to let the emotional weight of the moment sink in.

Learning Concepts

anger management, perseverance, growth mindset, creative thinking, problem solving

Vocabulary

magnificent, assistant, supplies, tinker, pounce, fiddle, nudge, adjust, examine, tweak, fasten, admirer, pummel, distraction, ward, alert

Discussion Prompts

- How did the girl and her dog work together as a team?
- Why do you think the girl became frustrated when her creations weren't perfect?
- What does this story teach us about trying and failing?
- How did taking a walk help the girl think differently about her project?
- Why is it important to have an assistant or a team when working on a big project?
- What are some of the skills (like measuring, building, experimenting) the girl used to create her magnificent thing?
- How do you think planning ahead helped the girl in her creation process?

- What do you think the story tells us about creativity and imagination?
- How did the girl's feelings change throughout the story and why?
- What could the girl have done differently when she first got frustrated?
- If you were the girl's assistant, what advice would you have given her?
- What did you learn from this story about perseverance and problem-solving?

Extension Activity

Students will bring the story to life by creating their own version of the girl's assistant, her faithful dog, and her inventive creation. After cutting out and assembling these paper pieces, students respond to a STEM-related writing prompt. This exercise not only enhances comprehension of the story but also encourages students to explore their imagination and develop their writing skills.

At-Home Extension

Discussion:
- Begin with a conversation about the book. Ask the child what they think made the girl's invention "magnificent" and discuss ideas for your own invention.

Design Phase:
- Together, sketch a design for your own "magnificent thing." It could be a vehicle, a gadget, or anything that sparks the child's imagination.

Gather Materials:
- Look for recyclable materials and craft supplies around the house that can be used to build your design.

Build Together:

- Work as a team to bring your design to life. The adult can handle more complex tasks like cutting cardboard, while the child can make creative decisions and do simpler tasks like gluing or decorating.

Reflection:

- After the activity, reflect on what you built. Discuss what parts were challenging, what you learned, and what was the most fun about the project.

Jabari Jumps

by Gaia Cornwall
Candlewick ©2020

The Story

An uplifting and beautifully illustrated story about a young boy, Jabari, who faces his fears of jumping off the diving board. The book captures the emotions of anticipation and bravery, resonating with anyone who's ever faced a personal challenge. Ideal for discussions about courage and growth, this story not only entertains with its relatable narrative but also imparts important lessons about trust, encouragement, and the pride that comes with overcoming fears. It's a heartening read that encourages children to take brave leaps, both big and small, in their lives.

Read-Aloud Tips

Character Voice and Emotion:
- Jabari: Give Jabari a voice filled with excitement and anticipation at the beginning, gradually changing to hesitation and nervousness as he approaches the diving board. When

he decides to jump, use a voice that conveys his newfound courage and accomplishment.

- Jabari's Father: Portray Jabari's father with a calm, encouraging, and supportive voice. His words are key to helping Jabari overcome his fear, so emphasize the kindness and patience in his voice.

Encouraging Empathy and Understanding: Throughout the reading, emphasize the moments where Jabari feels scared and how his father helps him. This can help children understand how to manage their fears and the role of supportive adults.

Learning Concepts

Bravery, sequencing, handling challenging situations

Vocabulary

diving board, stretches, rough, sprang, backflip

Discussion Prompts

- How did Jabari feel about the diving board at first?
- Can you remember what Jabari had completed before he decided to jump off the diving board?
- What reason did Jabari give for letting another kid go before him?
- Why did Jabari decide to take a tiny rest?
- How did Jabari's dad help him when he felt scared?
- What did Jabari do to make himself feel ready for the jump?
- How did Jabari feel when he finally stood at the end of the diving board?
- What was Jabari's reaction after he jumped into the water?
- Reflect on a time when you felt scared like Jabari, and how you overcame that fear.
- What advice would you give Jabari at the beginning of the story?

Extension Activity

After reading *Jabari Jumps* students will create a ladder using a provided template, symbolizing Jabari's climb. Inside this ladder, they are encouraged to write or draw three personal goals, mirroring Jabari's journey of overcoming fears and achieving his dream. This activity not only deepens their connection with the story but also fosters self-expression and goal-setting skills in a fun and engaging way.

At-Home Extension

This activity encourages children to explore their own goals and fears, inspired by Jabari's journey in *Jabari Jumps*. It also fosters communication, building on themes of courage, goal-setting, and overcoming obstacles.

Materials Needed:
- Paper and pencils or crayons
- Comfortable space for discussion

Instructions:

Reflection Discussion:
- Start with a conversation about the book. Ask the child what they thought about Jabari's experience and how they felt when he finally jumped. Discuss the concept of overcoming fears.

Identifying Personal Goals:
- Transition to discussing personal goals. Each person (adult and child) thinks of a goal they have, something they might be a bit afraid to try, just like Jabari was afraid to jump.

Drawing and Writing Session:
- Use paper and pencils or crayons to draw a picture of the goal. For children who can write, encourage them to write a sentence or two about their goal and what makes it a bit scary.

Storytelling Time:

- Each participant tells a short story about their drawing, imagining a successful outcome like Jabari's jump. Encourage the child to visualize overcoming their fear and achieving their goal.

Encouragement Exchange:

- End the activity by exchanging words of encouragement. Discuss how, like Jabari, it's okay to feel scared and how courage and support can help achieve goals.

Display the Artwork:

- Place the drawings in a visible spot as a reminder of the goals and the shared experience of the activity.

The Magical Yet

by Angela DiTerlizzi
Little, Brown Books for Young Readers ©2020

The Story

A whimsically illustrated and imaginative story that introduces a special creature, the Yet, symbolizing the potential within every child to achieve their goals, no matter the current challenges. This inspiring tale encourages young readers to embrace perseverance, growth mindset, and the power of "yet" in their abilities and dreams. The book not only entertains with its magical narrative but also teaches valuable lessons about patience, resilience, and the endless possibilities that await with time and practice. It's a delightful and motivating read that turns obstacles into opportunities for growth.

Read-Aloud Tips

Character Emotion and Voice: Portray the main character with a voice that reflects her journey from frustration to empowerment. Start with a tone of struggle or discouragement and gradually shift to excitement and confidence as she learns and grows. The "Yet" can be personified with a magical, encouraging, and gentle voice, almost like a fairy godmother, offering support and motivation.

Pacing and Tone: Use a slower pace and softer tone during the moments of frustration or challenge to emphasize the character's struggle. Gradually increase your pace and adopt a more upbeat and optimistic tone as the character begins to succeed, highlighting the positive transformation.

Utilizing Illustrations: Highlight the visual representation of the "Yet" as a fairy-like creature, drawing attention to how it symbolizes hope and possibility.

Learning Concepts

growth mindset, creative thinking, goal setting, problem-solving, perseverance

Vocabulary

wheelie, game changer, babble, schemer, kazoo, bassoon, tune, patient, bold

Discussion Prompts

- What does the "Magical Yet" represent in the story?
- What did the character learn from their experience with the bike?
- Can you think of a time when you learned something new after trying many times?
- Why is it important to keep trying, even when something is difficult?
- How does the "Magical Yet" help the character feel about challenges?
- What are some things you can do now that you couldn't do last year?
- How do you feel when you learn to do something you couldn't do before?

- What does the story teach us about making mistakes?
- Why is it okay to take a long time to learn something new?
- How does practicing something make you better at it?
- What would you say to a friend who is feeling frustrated about learning something new?
- How does the story of the "Magical Yet" make you feel about your future goals?

Extension Activity

This craftivity, designed to accompany the book *The Magical Yet*, provides a hands-on opportunity for students to explore the concepts of growth mindset and fixed mindset. Using a brain template, students will actively participate in differentiating between these two mindsets by sorting phrases into either the growth or fixed mindset side. This not only reinforces the book's themes but also encourages students to internalize the positive message of embracing challenges and persisting through difficulties.

At-Home Extension

Create a shared vision board that represents both of your aspirations, embodying the principles of growth mindset and goal-setting as inspired by *The Magical Yet*.

Materials Needed:
- A large poster board
- Magazines, newspapers, or printed images
- Coloring supplies
- Glue sticks or tape
- Stickers or decorative items
- Scissors

Instructions:

Read and Discuss:
- Begin by reading *The Magical Yet* together. Discuss the key themes of the book, focusing on how the "Yet" represents growth and learning through perseverance.

Brainstorming Session:

- Sit down with the child and brainstorm goals, dreams, and things you both wish to learn or achieve. Encourage the child to think about both short-term and long-term goals, and do the same for yourself.

Gather Materials:

- Look through magazines, newspapers, or online for images and words that represent these goals and aspirations.

Create the Vision Board:

- Start arranging and pasting these images and words onto the poster board. Divide the board into sections, if desired, to categorize different types of goals (e.g. personal, educational, hobbies). As you place each image, discuss how it relates to a growth mindset and the journey of achieving these goals.

Decorate and Personalize:

- Use markers, stickers, and other decorative items to personalize the vision board.

Reflection and Display:

- Once completed, spend some time reflecting on the vision board. Talk about how each element represents a step towards growth and learning. Hang the vision board in a common area where both of you can see it daily as a reminder of your shared journey towards achieving these goals.

We Are Water Protectors

by Carole Lindstrom

Roaring Brook Press ©2020

The Story

A beautifully illustrated and powerful story inspired by the many Indigenous-led movements across North America. It weaves a tale of a young girl who leads the fight to protect water and the Earth from harm. This book not only captivates with its vivid artwork and compelling narrative but also educates and inspires young readers about environmental stewardship, activism, and the importance of respecting and preserving nature. It's a poignant read that encourages children to consider their role in caring for the planet and standing up for what they believe in.

Read-Aloud Tips

Voice and Emotion: Give the Ojibwe girl a voice filled with determination and courage, reflecting her role as a protector of the water. Her voice should convey her passion for the cause and her connection to nature and her community. Portray the sense of urgency and the importance of the cause through your tone, emphasizing the seriousness of the environmental issues presented.

Pacing and Pauses: Use a deliberate pace to allow the weight of the words and the message to sink in. Employ strategic pauses, especially after poignant or powerful statements, to let the message resonate with the listeners.

Cultural Respect and Awareness: Highlight the cultural aspects of the story, discussing the significance of the Ojibwe people's connection to water and the land.

Learning Concepts

environmental awareness, cultural respect, critical thinking, nature

Vocabulary

nourish, sacred, rhythm, spoil, unfit, courage, rally, ancestor, steward

Discussion Prompts

- What is the main message of *We Are Water Protectors*?
- Name three ways water is important in the story.
- What is the black snake in the story, and what does it represent?
- Why is water called "the first medicine" in the book?
- How do the people in the story show that they are brave?
- What does it mean to be a water protector?
- Describe a time when you helped take care of nature.
- What can we learn from the story about taking care of the Earth?
- How does the story show that all living things are connected?
- Why do you think the author wrote this book?
- What are some ways we can keep water clean in our community?
- Why do you think it's important to stand up for what you believe in, like the characters in the book?
- How can you be a water protector in your daily life?
- If you could talk to the author, what would you ask or tell them about the book?

Extension Activity

This activity engages students in a creative and meaningful way by having them design their own water protector signs. Students will reflect on the important messages from *We Are Water Protectors* and express their understanding and passion for environmental stewardship.

At-Home Extension

Go on a water walk with your little learner to deepen understanding and appreciation of water's significance in our lives and community, inspired by the book *We Are Water Protectors*.

Preparation and Discussion:
- Before the walk, have a brief discussion about the book. Ask the child to recall the main themes and messages of *We Are Water Protectors*.
- Talk about the importance of water in your own lives and community. Discuss how you use water daily and why it's essential to protect it.

Planning the Route:
- Using a map, identify a nearby body of water–this could be a river, lake, stream, or even a pond in a local park.
- Plan a walking route that will take you to this body of water. The distance should be manageable for the child.

The Water Walk:
- As you walk, encourage the child to observe their surroundings. Look for signs of water in the environment, such as drainage systems, rainfall, plants that thrive in wet areas, and animals that depend on water.
- Discuss how this water might connect to larger water systems and the importance of keeping it clean and protected.

Observation and Reflection at the Water Source:

- Once you reach the water body, spend some time in quiet observation. What do you see, hear, and smell?
- Encourage the child to draw or write about their observations in a notebook. If they're interested, they can also take photographs.

Interactive Discussion:

- Discuss how this body of water is part of the larger ecosystem. Reflect on the story's themes and how they relate to what you see in front of you.
- Talk about the ways people might help protect this and other water sources.

Shark Lady: The True Story of How Eugenie Clark Became the Ocean's Most Fearless Scientist

by Jess Keating
Sourcebooks Explore ©2017

The Story

An inspiring and beautifully illustrated biography of Eugenie Clark, a pioneering marine biologist who challenged stereotypes and changed the world's perception of sharks. This captivating book not only introduces young readers to the wonders of marine biology but also celebrates the determination and curiosity of a woman who followed her dreams despite the odds. It's a powerful story that encourages children, especially girls, to explore science, overcome obstacles, and believe in the power of their dreams. It's a testament to the impact one person can have on understanding and protecting the natural world.

Read-Aloud Tips

Character Voices: Eugenie Clark: Portray Eugenie with a voice that reflects her curiosity, determination, and passion for sharks and the ocean. Use a tone of wonder and excitement when she talks about her discoveries.

Narrative Tone and Pacing: Use a tone of admiration and inspiration when narrating Eugenie's achievements and struggles. Adjust your pace to build excitement during her discoveries and reflect on the challenges she overcomes.

Learning Concepts

perseverance, marine biology, girl power, critical thinking, overcoming obstacles

Vocabulary

damp, constellation, speckle, current, daydream, margins, sanctuary, plunge, dispel, courage, mindless

Discussion Prompts

- Why did Eugenie want to stay at the aquarium forever?
- What kind of sharks did Eugenie learn about in her books?
- Why did some people tell Eugenie to forget about sharks?
- How did Eugenie prove her professors wrong about women being scientists?
- What myth about sharks did Eugenie dispel in Isla Mujeres?
- Why did people start calling Eugenie the "Shark Lady"?
- What did Eugenie prove about sharks and their intelligence?
- How did Eugenie's dream about sharks come true?
- Why is it important to follow your dreams, like Eugenie did?
- What can you learn from Eugenie about not giving up?
- How do you think Eugenie felt when others doubted her?

- If you could study any animal, like Eugenie studied sharks, which one would it be?
- What is one way you can start following your dream today, just like Eugenie?

Extension Activity

Get ready to embark on an underwater adventure that combines science, discovery, and inspiration! Inspired by the story of Eugenie, this activity is structured into four levels, each offering a deeper dive into the world of sharks, tailored to different learning stages. This activity not only educates students about these magnificent creatures but also encourages them to follow their dreams and persist in their interests, just like Eugenie did.

At-Home Extension

Enjoy a fun and educational day at the aquarium, inspired by Eugenie's love for marine life in the book *Shark Lady*. Participate in the following activities to make your visit more interactive!

Before the Aquarium Visit:
- Together, learn a few fun facts about sharks. Look at pictures or watch a short video about different types of sharks.

What to Look For:
- Talk about what you might see at the aquarium, like big sharks, colorful fish, and maybe even a turtle!

At the Aquarium:
- I Spy Game: Play a simple game of "I Spy" with marine animals. For example, "I spy something gray and big" for a shark.
- Find the Sharks: Make it a mission to find different types of sharks. Each time you see one, you can give a high-five!

Learning Through Play:

- Count the Fish: See how many fish you can count in one big tank. It's fun and helps with counting skills.
- Color Hunt: Look for fish that are red, blue, yellow, and other colors. It's like a rainbow underwater!

After the Aquarium Visit:

- Draw Your Favorite Fish: When you get home, draw pictures of your favorite fish or shark you saw at the aquarium.

First Day Jitters

by Julia Danneberg
Charlesbridge ©2000

The Story

A charming and relatable story that addresses the common nerves associated with new experiences, particularly the first day at a new school. Told with gentle humor and engaging illustrations, it captures the feelings of apprehension and excitement that come with change. Ideal for read-aloud sessions at the start of the school year, this book not only entertains with its surprise ending but also offers comfort and encouragement to children facing their own "first day jitters." It's a delightful read that encourages young readers to embrace new challenges and find joy in new beginnings.

Read-Aloud Tips

Set the Tone of Apprehension: Start with a slightly anxious tone to reflect the main character's nerves about the first day. This will help children relate to those familiar feelings of jitters.

Use Engaging Voices: Differentiate characters by giving them distinct voices. The main character might have a hesitant, worried tone, while supportive characters can have cheerful, reassuring voices.

Emphasize Illustrations: Pause to let the children absorb the illustrations, pointing out details that highlight the character's emotions. Ask them what they think the character is feeling at that moment.

Encourage Empathy: As you read about the character's worries, invite the children to share their own first-day experiences. Ask questions like, "What are you nervous about on your first day?"

Build Suspense: When the story reaches the climax, create a sense of suspense by reading slowly and using dramatic pauses. This keeps the children engaged and anticipating the surprise ending.

Learning Concepts

developing empathy, embracing change, recognizing support systems such as friendship

Vocabulary

stumble, fumble, trudge, slump, peek

Discussion Prompts

- Why did Sarah want to stay in bed?
- How did Sarah feel about starting over at a new school?
- What physical signs showed that Sarah was nervous?
- How did Mrs. Burton, the principal, react when she saw Sarah in the car?
- What was Sarah's impression of the school as she walked through the hallways?

- Can you remember a time when you were nervous about something new? How did it feel?
- How did Mrs. Burton introduce Sarah to the class?
- What was the big twist at the end of the story?
- How do you think the students felt when they found out Sarah was their new teacher?
- Why do you think the author chose to surprise the readers with the twist?
- How does the story show that both kids and adults can feel nervous about new things?
- If you were in Sarah's position, how would you have felt about your first day?
- What did you learn from this story about trying new things and dealing with nervousness?

Extension Activity

As an interactive way to enhance students' comprehension of *First Day Jitters*, this sequencing activity invites them to dive deeper into the story's narrative. By cutting and pasting events in the correct order, students not only reinforce their understanding of the plot but also develop critical thinking and story analysis skills. This hands-on activity is perfect for reinforcing key concepts!

At-Home Extension

Making the daunting prospect of the first day of school a bit more approachable and less intimidating! Help your children express and manage their nervous feelings about the first day of school in a creative and tangible way with this Worry Box activity.

Materials:
- Shoebox
- Coloring Materials/Decorative Materials
- Paper

Instructions:

Discuss the Story:
- Start by reading *First Day Jitters* together. Talk about how Sarah felt nervous about her first day and how those feelings are normal. Discuss if the child has any similar feelings about their first day.

Create the Worry Monster Box:
- Take the small box and encourage the child to turn it into a "Worry Monster." They can cover it with construction paper or fabric, use markers or paint to decorate it, and add features like googly eyes, teeth, and ears. The idea is to make it fun and engaging.

Write Down Worries:
- On the small strips of paper or sticky notes, have the child write down or draw any worries or fears they have about the first day of school. This can include meeting new people, finding their classroom, or anything else on their mind.

Feed the Worry Monster:
- One by one, let the child "feed" their worries to the Worry Monster by placing the notes inside the box. Explain that the Worry Monster is there to hold onto their fears so they don't have to.

Discussion and Reassurance:
- As each worry is fed to the monster, discuss it briefly. Offer reassurance, and share any personal experiences or advice about overcoming similar worries. This is an opportunity to validate their feelings and help them see that they are not alone in their concerns.

Place the Box in a Special Place:
- Finally, find a special place to keep the Worry Monster, like next to their bed or in a spot in their room. Encourage the child to add new worries anytime, and revisit the box periodically to talk about whether those worries have lessened or changed.

Our Class Is a Family

by Shannon Olsen
Shannon Olsen ©2020

The Story

A heartwarming and beautifully illustrated story that celebrates the special bond formed within a classroom community. It emphasizes the idea that a class is more than just a group of students; it's a family where everyone belongs and is valued. Perfect for read-aloud sessions in the classroom to start the year, this book not only fosters a sense of belonging and inclusivity but also teaches important values like kindness, cooperation, and respect. It's an uplifting read that reinforces the message that in a classroom, everyone can find a place where they feel safe, supported, and part of a caring community.

Read-Aloud Tips

Set a Warm Tone: Start with a gentle, welcoming voice to convey the warmth of the classroom community. This sets a positive atmosphere that resonates with the themes of belonging and inclusivity.

Highlight Illustrations: Pause to allow children to absorb the beautiful illustrations. Encourage them to notice how the characters interact and express their feelings, reinforcing the idea of family within the classroom.

Use Character Voices: Differentiate characters with varied tones to bring their personalities to life. For example, use a cheerful voice for the supportive characters and a softer, more introspective tone for those expressing their feelings of uncertainty.

Encourage Participation: Invite students to share their thoughts about what makes their class feel like a family. Ask questions like, "What do you think it means to be part of a family?" to foster engagement and connection.

Emphasize Key Messages: As you read, highlight important values such as kindness and cooperation. Use repetition to reinforce these messages, encouraging children to remember them.

Create a Sense of Community: Encourage the children to think of ways they can contribute to their classroom family. Ask them to suggest acts of kindness they could perform for classmates.

Learning Concepts

creating community, cooperation, friendship

Vocabulary

related, connection, unique, haven, peer,

Discussion Prompts

- What does the phrase "Our class is a family" mean to you?
- Name three ways our classroom is like a family.
- Why do you think it's important to treat classmates like family members?
- How can we show kindness to our classmates, like we do in a family?
- What does respect look like in our classroom? Can you give an example?

- How can we celebrate each other's differences in our class?
- Why is it important to listen to your classmates' ideas and thoughts?
- What can you do if you see a classmate feeling sad or left out?
- How do you feel on the first day of school and how can our class family help?
- What does it mean to be a good friend in our classroom family?
- How can working together help us learn better in our class?
- What are some ways we can support each other when things are tough?
- What makes our classroom a special place for you?
- If you could add one rule to make our class even more like a family, what would it be?
- What are you most excited about learning this year with our classroom family?

Extension Activity

Kick off the school year, helping students feel connected and valued in their new classroom family! This activity is designed to foster a sense of community and belonging in the classroom. Students will creatively assemble parts of a school building, mirroring the book's cover. Inside this structure, they'll respond to prompts through drawings or written words. This not only serves as a meaningful learning experience but also transforms into an eye-catching back-to-school bulletin board, celebrating our classroom's diversity and togetherness.

At-Home Extension

After reading *Our Class Is a Family*, engage in meaningful activity that reinforces the themes of the book. The activity involves creating a "Classroom Family Tree" which celebrates the diversity and uniqueness of each class member, including the child and their teacher.

Materials Needed:
- Poster board
- Coloring supplies
- Stickers (optional)

Instructions:

Discuss the Concept:
- Start by discussing with the child how each classmate, like a family member, plays a unique and important role in their classroom community. Emphasize the value of everyone's differences and similarities.

Draw the Tree:
- On the poster board, draw a large tree with enough branches to represent each member of the child's class, including the teacher.

Add Class Members:
- Assign a branch to each classmate. The child can either draw their classmates and teacher or use photos if available. They can also write their names under each picture.

Personalize the Tree:
- Encourage the child to decorate the tree with drawings or stickers that represent different qualities of their classroom family, like kindness, teamwork, and diversity.

Share Stories:
- As they add each classmate to the tree, the child can share something special about that person or a fond memory they have with them.

Display the Family Tree:
- Once completed, find a special place at home to display the "Classroom Family Tree" or bring it into school! It serves as a reminder of the supportive and caring environment they have at school.

Discussion and Reflection:
- Conclude the activity with a discussion about what they learned and how they feel being part of their classroom family.

Chrysanthemum

by Kevin Henkes
Greenwillow Books ©2020

The Story

A sweet and engaging story about a young girl who learns to embrace the uniqueness of her name and herself, despite teasing from her classmates. With charming illustrations and a narrative that captures the emotions of wanting to fit in, this book beautifully addresses themes of self-esteem and the power of kind words. Ideal for read-aloud sessions and classroom discussions, it not only entertains with its relatable storyline but also imparts valuable lessons about appreciating one's own uniqueness and the importance of empathy and support from others. It's a heartening read that encourages children to celebrate their individuality and the beauty in being different.

Read-Aloud Tips

Express Chrysanthemum's Emotions: Use your voice to reflect Chrysanthemum's changing emotions—start with her excitement and pride about her name, then shift to a more downcast tone as she experiences teasing, and finally, end with confidence and joy as she learns to embrace her uniqueness.

Differentiate Character Voices: Use distinct voices for the different characters—make the teasing classmates sound dismissive or mocking, while Chrysanthemum's parents and the supportive teacher have warm, reassuring tones to highlight the importance of kindness and empathy.

Highlight the Illustrations: Point out Chrysanthemum's body language and facial expressions in the illustrations to help children recognize how she feels at different points in the story. This adds depth to the narrative and encourages empathy.

Pause for Reflection: After key moments, like when Chrysanthemum is teased or supported, pause and ask the children how they think she feels. This engages them emotionally and opens up a discussion about how words can impact others.

Encourage Participation: Ask children to share their own names and the meanings or stories behind them. This activity fosters a sense of pride in individuality and helps children relate to Chrysanthemum's journey.

Learning Concepts

Celebrating individuality, embracing change, developing empathy

Vocabulary

scarcely, wilt, dreadful, inform, precious, priceless, fascinating, pleasant, envious, begrudge, jaundice, trifle, sprout, prized, possessions, indescribable, scales, dainty, spiffy, beam

Discussion Prompts

- How did Chrysanthemum feel about her name before she started school?

- How did the other students react when they first heard Chrysanthemum's name?
- Why did Chrysanthemum start to dislike her name at school?
- How did Chrysanthemum's parents comfort her after her first day at school?
- How did Chrysanthemum's feelings change after the music teacher, Mrs. Twinkle, talked about her own name?
- What did Chrysanthemum dream about the night after her first day at school? What does this say about how she was feeling?
- How did the other students change their behavior towards Chrysanthemum after Mrs. Twinkle shared her name?
- What lesson did Chrysanthemum learn about being different?
- How did the character of Mrs. Twinkle influence Chrysanthemum's experience at school?
- Why do you think Chrysanthemum's parents chose that name for her?
- What would you do if you were in Chrysanthemum's situation at school?
- How did Chrysanthemum feel when she heard Mrs. Twinkle's baby's name?
- Why is it important to be kind to others who are different from us?

Extension Activity

Blend art, literacy, and self-reflection in your classroom! After reading *Chrysanthemum* students will cut and paste to create their own version of the charming character Chrysanthemum. This activity reinforces the story's themes and sets the stage for a reflective writing prompt. After crafting their Chrysanthemum, students delve into a personal exploration about their own names, encouraging them to connect with the story on a deeper level and celebrate the uniqueness of their identities.

At-Home Extension

Create acrostic poems to promote a deeper appreciation of each other's unique traits and qualities. It's a wonderful way to bond and create lasting memories through the power of words.

Materials Needed:
- Paper
- Pencil
- Coloring supplies (optional)

Instructions:

Introduction to Acrostic Poems:
- Begin by explaining what an acrostic poem is.
- An acrostic poem is a type of poetry where the first letter of each line spells out a word or message, usually related to the subject of the poem. In this case, the subject will be the names of the participants.

Selecting Names:
- Each participant (both adult and child) chooses their own name or a nickname they cherish. Write these names vertically down the left side of a piece of paper, one letter per line.

Brainstorming Session:
- Spend some time brainstorming words or phrases that start with each letter of the names. These can include characteristics they like about themselves, their interests, or anything positive or meaningful. A dictionary or thesaurus can be handy here to find new and exciting words.

Creating the Poem:
- Using the brainstormed list, start crafting sentences or phrases for each letter of the name. Remember, each line of the poem should start with the corresponding letter from the name and should reflect something about the person.

Sharing and Discussion:
- Once both participants have completed their poems, take turns reading them aloud. Discuss what each line and the overall poem reveal about each person's personality, interests, and values.

Decoration and Display:
- If desired, decorate the poems with drawings, stickers, or other craft materials. Display the completed acrostic poems in a shared space as a reminder of the unique qualities each person brings to their relationship.

The Kissing Hand

by Audrey Penn
Tanglewood ©2020

The Story

A tender and reassuring story that addresses the common child-hood anxiety of separation, especially when starting school. Through the tale of a young raccoon and his mother, it introduces the concept of an invisible bond of love that connects loved ones, no matter the distance. Ideal for read-aloud sessions, particularly during transitions like starting school, this book not only comforts with its sweet narrative and gentle illustrations but also teaches children that they carry their loved ones' love with them wherever they go. It's a touching read that provides solace and confidence to children facing new experiences.

Read-Aloud Tips

Use a Soft, Soothing Tone: Begin with a calming voice to reflect the tender nature of the story, emphasizing the reas-suring bond between the raccoon and its mother. This sets the tone for the comforting message of the book.

Express the Emotions: Bring out the raccoon's nervousness and the mother's loving reassurance. Use slight tremors in your voice to convey the raccoon's anxiety and a warm, steady tone to reflect the mother's comforting presence.

Pause for Reflection: After reading about the "kissing hand" moment, pause to let the significance of that gesture sink in. Ask children how they feel when they miss someone and what helps them feel better.

Use Gestures: As you read about the mother kissing her child's hand, invite children to mimic the gesture, encouraging them to imagine someone they love doing the same. This adds a personal and interactive element to the story.

Encourage Empathy: Discuss feelings of separation and anxiety, encouraging children to share their own experiences with new situations like starting school. Validate their feelings and emphasize that it's okay to feel nervous.

Learning Concepts

Life transitions, embracing change, facing fear, independence

Vocabulary

nuzzle, palm, silky, tingle, grin, scamper, limb

Discussion Prompts

- Why was Chester the raccoon crying at the beginning of the story?
- How did Mrs. Raccoon react when Chester said he didn't want to go to school?
- Why do you think Mrs. Raccoon told Chester that sometimes we have to do things we don't want to do?
- Have you ever been scared to try something new like Chester? What were you scared or nervous about? How did it turn out in the end?
- What was the "Kissing Hand"?

- How did Chester feel when his mother gave him the Kissing Hand?
- When Chester felt lonely at school, what could he do with his hand to feel better?
- Do you have a special way to remember someone's love, like the Kissing Hand?
- How did the Kissing Hand help Chester?
- Why do you think Chester gave his mother a Kissing Hand too?
- How did Mrs. Raccoon feel after Chester gave her the Kissing Hand?
- How did Chester's feelings about school change from the beginning of the book to the end?
- What was the main message of the story, and how could you apply it in your own life?

Extension Activity

This creative activity allows students to explore the themes of love and comfort through art and writing. Students create a unique heart representing the "Kissing Hand." On one side of this heart, they will create a visual representation of two thumbprints coming together. On the reverse side, they are encouraged to express their feelings by either drawing a picture or writing a letter to someone they love. This activity reinforces the story's message and provides a meaningful way for students to connect with their emotions and share their affection for loved ones.

At-Home Extension

After reading *The Kissing Hand* with your child, engage in a special activity to deepen the connection with the book's theme and create a lasting memory. This art activity is a fun and meaningful way to explore the concepts of love, comfort, and reassurance, especially in times of separation or new experiences.

Materials Needed:
- Ink pad or markers
- Paper

Instructions:

Create Your Kissing Hands:
- If you have an ink pad, start by pressing each of your thumbs onto it. If you don't have an ink pad, you can alternatively color your thumbs with a washable marker. Then, press your inked or colored thumbs onto a piece of paper, creating two thumbprints side by side in the shape of a heart. Do this for both the parent and the child, creating two sets of "Kissing Hands."

Decorate and Personalize:
- Once the thumbprint hearts are created, decorate around them. You can draw, use stickers, or write messages. Encourage your child to express their creativity.

Exchange of Hearts:
- When both of you have finished, exchange your "Kissing Hands" papers. This exchange symbolizes the sharing of love and comfort, just like in the story.

Discussion:
- Talk about the feelings associated with the "Kissing Hand." Ask your child how they feel when they think about the love and care of their family, especially in new or challenging situations.

Display Your Artwork:
- Find a special place in your home to display these "Kissing Hands." They can serve as a reminder of your bond and the comfort you provide each other, especially when apart.

The Day You Begin

by Jacqueline Woodson
Nancy Paulsen Books ©2018

The Story

A moving and beautifully illustrated story that speaks to the experience of feeling different and finding the courage to connect with others. This narrative, rich in diversity and empathy, encourages young readers to embrace their unique stories and discover the beauty in sharing them. Ideal for read-aloud sessions and discussions about inclusivity and self-acceptance, this book not only captivates with its lyrical prose but also imparts important lessons about the power of vulnerability and the strength found in coming together. It's an inspiring and heartwarming read that celebrates the courage to be oneself and the joy of finding common ground with others.

Read-Aloud Tips

Set a Reflective Tone: Begin with a calm, thoughtful voice to reflect the introspective nature of the story. As the narrative unfolds, use your tone to convey both the uncertainty and eventual empowerment the characters feel.

Highlight Diversity: Emphasize the descriptions of different backgrounds and experiences to help children appreciate the beauty in diversity. As you read, ask the audience to think about what makes them unique and how their stories can be celebrated.

Voice the Vulnerability: Use a soft, slightly hesitant tone when characters express their fears of being different, then transition to a more confident tone as they begin to connect with others. This will help children follow the emotional journey of the story.

Encourage Personal Connection: Pause at key moments and ask open-ended questions like, "Have you ever felt like you didn't belong?" or "What makes you feel special?" This encourages children to relate their own experiences to the characters.

Use the Illustrations: Draw attention to the vibrant illustrations that visually represent each character's unique background. Point out details in the pictures that enhance the storytelling and help young readers see the diversity in the characters.

Learning Concepts

embracing diversity, respecting individuality, developing empathy

Vocabulary

homeland, fragile, souvenir, curb, kimchi, steel

Discussion Prompts

- What did you feel when you first heard the story of *The Day You Begin*?
- How did the characters in the book feel when they were in a room where no one was quite like them?
- What did you think about when the book talked about different languages and the beauty of words?
- Can you remember a time when you moved to a new place or started at a new school? How did you feel then?
- How did the main character feel when hearing about the travels and adventures of other children?
- What do you think about the different lunches mentioned in the book, like rice and kimchi? Have you tried foods from other cultures?
- How can we be welcoming to someone who eats different food than we do?
- What did Angelina do over the summer that was special, even though she didn't travel far?
- What does the story teach us about finding things in common with others?
- What are some ways we can make new students feel welcome in our classroom?
- How can we celebrate the things that make each of us unique?
- What did you learn from *The Day You Begin* about being brave and sharing your story?

Extension Activity

This creative and inclusive exercise is designed to encourage students to express and share their unique stories, just as the characters in the book do. By drawing or writing about themselves inside a brochure, students create a personal snapshot of who they are. This activity not only serves as a fun "get to know me" project but also fosters a sense of belonging and community in the classroom. Teachers can invite students to voluntarily share their brochures, further promoting a culture of openness and acceptance in your class.

At-Home Extension

Create a bonding experience between an adult and a child through shared storytelling, inspired by *The Day You Begin*. This activity aims to encourage open communication, celebrate diversity, and build a collection of cherished memories.

Materials Needed:
- A clear jar or container
- Small pieces of paper or colorful note cards
- Pens or markers

Instructions:

Set Up:
- Sit together in a comfortable space with the jar, paper, and pens at hand.
- Explain the purpose of the activity: to share stories and experiences, just like in *The Day You Begin*.

Sharing Stories:
- Take turns to share stories about your lives. These can be about anything—a memorable day, a difficult challenge you overcame, a favorite holiday, your cultural background, or even dreams and aspirations.

Writing and Collecting Memories:
- After each story is shared, both the adult and the child write a short summary or key point from the story on a piece of paper.
- Fold the paper and place it in the jar. These are your "memory notes."

Reflection:

- Discuss how it felt to share and listen to each other's stories. Emphasize the importance of understanding and celebrating each other's unique experiences, just like the characters in the book.
- Talk about any new things you learned about each other or any surprising commonalities you discovered.

Continuing the Activity:

- Keep the jar in a common area of your home.
- Make a habit of adding new stories to the jar regularly—it could be weekly or during special moments or holidays.
- Periodically, perhaps at the end of the year or on special occasions, open the jar and read the memories together, reliving and cherishing these shared moments.

Amy Wu and the Warm Welcome

by Kat Zhang

Simon & Schuster Books for Young Readers ©2022

The Story

An endearing and vibrantly illustrated story that follows Amy Wu as she navigates the challenges and joys of helping a new student in her class feel welcome. This delightful tale explores themes of friendship, inclusivity, and the importance of cultural sensitivity. Ideal for classroom read-alouds and discussions, the book not only entertains with its engaging narrative but also teaches valuable lessons about kindness, empathy, and the power of reaching out to make everyone feel included. It's an uplifting and educational read that celebrates the richness of diverse friendships and the positive impact of a warm welcome.

Read-Aloud Tips

Bring Amy's Emotions to Life: As Amy navigates the uncertainty of welcoming a new student, use a range of tones to express her curiosity, excitement, and moments of hesitation.

Show her growing confidence as she learns to connect with her new friend.

Emphasize Inclusivity: When reading the moments where Amy and her classmates help the new student, highlight the words that reflect empathy and kindness. Pause to ask children how they would make a new student feel welcome, encouraging participation.

Use Cultural Sensitivity: When discussing the new student's cultural background, speak with respect and interest. Draw attention to any cultural elements in the illustrations, fostering a positive conversation about diversity.

Highlight Friendship: As the new friendship forms, let your tone become warmer and more joyful. Use this shift to convey the happiness that comes from making new friends and building connections.

Interactive Questions: Encourage children to think about times when they had to help someone new or were new themselves. Ask, "What's something kind you could do to welcome someone?"

Learning Concepts

showing kindness, community building, friendship

Vocabulary

welcome, grin, dumpling, tangerine, aboard, chatter, ponder, characters, banner

Discussion Prompts

- How did Amy react when she first saw Lin at school?
- Describe Lin's reaction when he was welcomed by Amy's class.
- What did Lin eat for lunch and how did this connect to Amy's plans for the evening?

- In what ways did Amy try to make Lin feel included during playtime?
- What was Amy's reaction to Lin's silence during show and tell?
- Describe the change in Lin's behavior when his family arrived at school.
- How did Amy's observation of Lin with his family influence her understanding of him?
- What did Amy ponder while shopping with her mom and how did it lead to her plan?
- How did Amy's grandma help her with her plan to welcome Lin?
- Describe Amy's feelings and actions as she waited for guests with her banner.
- How did Amy's inability to speak out loud during the party make her feel?
- What did Lin do to help Amy when she struggled to speak?
- What realization did Amy have when it was time for Lin to go home?
- Reflect on a time when you felt like Lin, the new person in a group. How did others make you feel welcome?
- Think about a time when someone new joined your class or group. How did you contribute to making them feel welcome?

Extension Activity

In this creative and culturally enriching activity, students will explore the concept of welcoming through the universal language of food. Encourage students to draw a meal that they would serve to someone new, as a way to make them feel welcomed and included. This activity fosters empathy and understanding. It also allows students to express their own cultural heritage or culinary interests.

At-Home Extension

Promote cultural awareness and appreciation by exploring greetings in various languages. It's a fun and educational way to bond after reading Amy Wu and the Warm Welcome.

Materials Needed:
- Internet access
- Coloring materials

Instructions:

Research Together:
- Start by looking up how to say "hello" in different languages. You can choose languages from countries you are curious about, or perhaps pick languages based on countries represented in your community or family heritage.

Create a Language Chart:
- On a sheet of paper, write down each language and its corresponding greeting. For example, "Spanish-Hola," "Mandarin-你好 (Nǐ hǎo)," "French-Bonjour." Use markers or crayons to add colors or flags next to each language for a more vibrant and informative chart.

Practice Time:
- Take turns with the child practicing each greeting. Make it more engaging by pretending to meet each other for the first time in each different language.

Discussion:
- Discuss how it feels to say hello in different languages. Ask questions like, "Which greeting was your favorite and why?" or "How do you think saying hello in different languages can make someone new feel welcome?"

Extend the Learning (Optional):
- If you have a globe or world map, you can locate the countries where each language is spoken. This adds a geographical element to the learning experience.

Oh, the Places You'll Go

by Dr. Seuss
Random House Books for Young Readers ©1990

The Story

An inspiring and beautifully illustrated Dr. Seuss classic that cel-ebrates life's journey with its ups and downs, encouraging young readers to seize life's opportunities and navigate its challenges with courage and optimism. This whimsical and wise tale is perfect for read-aloud sessions, graduations, or moments of transition, offer-ing not only entertainment with its playful rhymes and imaginative landscapes but also imparting invaluable life lessons about resil-ience, self-discovery, and the endless possibilities that await. It's a timeless and uplifting read that motivates readers of all ages to embark on their own adventures with confidence and curiosity.

Read-Aloud Tips

Emphasize the Rhythmic Flow: Dr. Seuss's playful rhymes are central to the story's charm. Keep a steady rhythm while reading, but vary your pacing to match the emotional shifts in the narrative—slowing down during moments of reflection and speeding up during more adventurous sections.

Highlight Life's Ups and Downs: Use your tone and inflection to emphasize the contrast between life's highs (exciting opportunities, fun adventures) and lows (challenges, uncertain times). This helps convey the full range of emotions present in the story.

Encourage Participation: Ask listeners how they would navigate their own journey. Pause at key moments to encourage children to imagine their own paths and what choices they might make in similar situations.

Use Dramatic Pauses: Seuss's writing often features moments that call for a reflective pause—such as before big decisions or when facing challenges. Give these moments weight by pausing to let the message sink in.

Bring the Illustrations to Life: As you read about the whimsical landscapes and vivid scenes, describe what's happening in the illustrations with enthusiasm. This draws listeners deeper into Seuss's imaginative world.

Learning Concepts

resilience, problem-solving, self-discovery, courage

Vocabulary

brainy, sights, soar, perch, lurch, slump, sprain, quarters, lowly, foul, prowl, dexterous, deft, succeed, guaranteed

Discussion Prompts

- How did the character feel when they started their journey?
- What kind of challenges did the character face in the story?
- Can you describe a time when you felt excited about going somewhere new, like the character in the book?
- What did the character learn about making choices?
- How did the character handle difficult situations?
- What does the phrase "You're off to Great Places!" mean to you?
- What does the book teach you about facing problems?

- How can you relate the character's journey to the end of your school year?
- What are some dreams or goals you have, like the character in the book?
- What do you think it means to be "brainy and footsy" like the character?
- What places would you like to go to after this school year ends?
- Why do you think it's important to keep going, even when things are tough?
- How do you think you can overcome challenges at school or in life?
- Why do you think the book says, "You'll move mountains"?
- How did the character change from the beginning to the end of the book?
- How can you use what you learned this school year to help you in new situations?
- What are you looking forward to doing or achieving after this school year?

Extension Activity

This activity complements the inspiring themes of *Oh, the Places You'll Go!* by Dr. Seuss. Students express their creativity and aspirations by designing their own hot air balloon, reminiscent of the ones in the story. As they color and personalize their balloons, encourage them to think deeply about the places they dream of visiting or the goals they aspire to achieve. This activity not only fosters artistic expression but also allows students to articulate and visualize their future aspirations.

At-Home Extension

Embark on a creative journey with your child after reading Dr. Seuss's *Oh, the Places You'll Go!* by engaging in the "Future Me" drawing activity. This simple and fun exercise encourages your child to imagine and illustrate their aspirations for the future, fostering both creativity and discussion about their dreams and goals.

It's a wonderful way to bond and soar deeper into the themes of the book while celebrating your child's imagination.

Materials Needed:
- Coloring supplies
- Paper

Discuss the Book:
- Begin by talking about the book. Ask your child about their favorite part of the story and how the character explored different places and faced challenges.

Imagine the Future:
- Encourage your child to imagine where they might go and what they might do in the future. Ask questions like, "What do you want to be when you grow up?" or "Is there a place you dream of visiting?"

Draw the "Future Me":
- Give your child a sheet of paper and some coloring materials. Ask them to draw themselves in the future, doing something they aspire to or in a place they wish to visit. This could be anything from being an astronaut to visiting a famous landmark.

Describe the Drawing:
- Once they finish their drawing, have your child describe it to you. Listen as they explain what they drew and why they chose that particular scene.

Display the Artwork:
- Find a spot in your home where you can display their "Future Me" drawing. This can be a proud reminder of their aspirations and the fun they had imagining their future.

Index